MW01128264

To my mom,

Juddean Ferguson Creasy Kauble,

Mother Bunny Extraordinaire

Do not remember the former things

nor consider the things of old.

I am about to do a new thing;

now it springs forth,

do you not perceive it?

Isaiah 43:19

Endorsements

This is the book the Church has been waiting for. Kenda Creasy Dean leads us humbly to discover love's relentless creativity and imagines a new kind of flourishing. *Innovating for Love* quickens us to love as we are loved. Indeed, our collective grief has loosened us to receive her timely invitation, to embody God's new thing. We are all hungry for this message.

Gregory Boyle
Founder, Homeboy Industries • Author, *Tattoos On The Heart*

Kenda Dean knows exactly what time it is in the church. It is time to come to terms with our common weariness about a church that is excessively compromised and accommodated to culture. More than that, it is time to let the deep mandate of love energize new entrepreneurial efforts to explore new ways of ministry. Dean is utterly serious and completely convinced that the church, because of its singular mandate to love, can indeed be innovative in ways that add real value to human life, citing numerous specific examples of innovative church initiatives and an extended battery of "practices" in the art of innovation. Dean invites us to a fresh breath in the church that is nothing less than the gift of the Spirit.

Walter Brueggemann
Columbia Theological Seminary

If you're a young person, congregant or pastor teetering between whether or not to practice innovation, Kenda Creasy Dean argues compellingly why you and your church should be all in, and articulates beautifully a theology and rationale for why Christians innovate. If your curiosity is piqued, read the evocative words of this professorial innovator. Invite others to practice the ideas in this engaging work of art. And be inspired to see, think about, and approach Christian ministry and service as an innovative expression of God's love for us all.

Stephen Lewis
President of the Forum for Theological Exploration
Co-author of *Another Way: Living and Leading Change on Purpose*

Dean flips the script on Christian social innovation and explains why fear cannot be at the root of effective change. With wit, wisdom and well-honed experience, Dean challenges our imaginations and empowers faithful leaders to mine their communities and traditions for the creativity and innovation already present in them. This practical, applicable and creative collection will transform the way churches, Christian communities and their leaders love their way into new and renewed expressions of God's love for the world.

Victoria Atkinson White
Managing Director of Grants, Leadership Education at Duke Divinity School

Innovating for Love provided me with a course correction. After years of thinking about the need for change in churches, I'd fallen prey to the notion that Christian social innovation was all about identifying and realizing a creative idea. This book kindly – yet strongly, authoritatively – realigned my thinking toward a better motivation and approach.

Mark Oestreicher
Founder and Partner, The Youth Cartel

A must-read for all church leaders. As the world increasingly calls for expediency and re-invention, Kenda Creasy Dean cuts through the "innovation" lingo, and does here what she does best: she accompanies faith leaders, and wonders with them about innovation in the Church. Nudging us along with clarity, humility, hope, and practical ideas, Dean reminds us that love-infused innovation is the stuff of Jesus. And it can save the Church, one locale at a time.

Rev. Jill Olds
Director of the Yale Youth Ministry Institute

Innovating for Love is for anyone who loves the church, hates the church, is disillusioned by the church, or just wants their faith to matter. Dean disorients without paralyzing, is practical without being prescriptive, and leaves readers seeing their world differently. Drawing deeply from Scripture as well as the ongoing story of the church, this is the book to read on Christian innovation.

Rev. Dr. Amanda Drury
Associate Professor of Practical Theology, Indiana Wesleyan University
Founder, "Discipleship by Design"

I love innovation even more after reading *Innovating for Love*. My dear friend Kenda masterfully offers what every leader hungers for: a Jesus-centered journey to fresh ministry fueled by love, mission, and hope. In her typical ministry savvy, Kenda pairs that powerful vision with the generative case studies and practical ideas you and I need to take our next faithful steps forward.

Kara Powell, PhD
Chief of Leadership Formation at Fuller Seminary
Executive Director of the Fuller Youth Institute

Innovating for Love

Joining God's Expedition through

Christian Social Innovation

Kenda Creasy Dean

Innovating for Love

Joining God's Expedition through

Christian Social Innovation

©2022 Kenda Creasy Dean

books@marketsquarebooks.com
141 N. Martinwood Rd. Knoxville TN 37923
ISBN: 978-1-950899-55-5

Printed and Bound in the United States of America
Cover Illustration & Book Design ©2021 Market Square Publishing, LLC

Editor: Charlie Langford
Contributing Editor: Kay Kotan

All rights reserved. No part of this book may be reproduced in any
manner without written permission except in the case of brief quotations
included in critical articles and reviews. For information, please contact
Market Square Publishing, LLC.

Unless noted, Scripture quotations are from:

NRSV

New Revised Standard Version Bible,
copyright © 1989 National Council of the Churches of Christ
in the United States of America.
Used by permission. All rights reserved worldwide.

This resource was commissioned as
one of many interconnected steps in the
journey of *The Greatest Expedition*.

GreatestExpedition.com

Table of Contents

Foreword

This resource was commissioned as one of many interconnected steps in the journey of *The Greatest Expedition*. While each step is important individually, we intentionally built the multi-step Essentials Pack and the Expansion Pack to provide a richer and fuller experience with the greatest potential for transformation and introducing more people to a relationship with Jesus Christ. For more information, visit GreatestExpedition.org.

However, we also recognize you may be exploring this resource apart from *The Greatest Expedition*. You might find yourself on a personal journey, a small group journey, or perhaps a church leadership team journey. We are so glad you are on this journey!

As you take each step in your expedition, your Expedition Team will discover whether the ministry tools you will be exploring will be utilized only for the Expedition Team or if this expedition will be a congregational journey. Our hope and prayer is *The Greatest Expedition* is indeed a congregational journey, but if it proves to be a solo journey for just the Expedition Team, God will still do amazing things through your intentional exploration, discernment, and faithful next steps.

Regardless of how you came to discover *The Greatest*

Expedition, it will pave the way to a new God-inspired expedition. Be brave and courageous on your journey through *The Greatest Expedition!*

Kay L Kotan, PCC
Director, *The Greatest Expedition*

INTRODUCTION

Why Innovation is
the Wrong Word[1]

In his famous TED talk, author and former ad man Simon Sinek argues that the genius of successful companies is that they start with why. Unlike most of us, who try to win a hearing by explaining what our organization does, world-class innovators like Steve Jobs start with the purpose that motivates them: what is the purpose of an iPhone in the first place? "People don't buy what you do," maintains Sinek, "they buy why you do it." He describes ordinary sales pitches like this: "We make great computers [what]. They're beautifully designed, simple to use, and user-friendly [how]. Wanna buy one?" He contrasts this with inspiring pitches that lead with a company's purpose, like Apple: "We believe in thinking differently [why]. The way we do that is by making our products beautifully designed, simple to use, and user-friendly [how]. We just happen to make great computers [what]. Wanna buy one?"[2]

Sinek's TED talk is compelling. It has been viewed more than 56,000,000 times. It's the third-most-watched TED talk of all time. The only problem is that Sinek is wrong.

---

1   I am grateful to Dr. Wesley Ellis; our conversations about a theological role for innovation in the church has shaped my thinking on this point in particular.

2   Simon Sinek, "Starting with Why" (September 2009), https://www.ted.com/talks/simon_sinek_how_great_leaders_inspire_action?language=en (accessed April 7, 2021).

Don't Start with Why – Start with Who

"Why" matters to ministry. It is devastatingly important to align, to the best of our ability, our purposes with God's purposes, so that our bottom line does not become our plumb line. But Jesus' ministry started with who, not why – with the person in front of him, in all their sweaty, frayed humanity. Before he embodied ministry, Jesus embodied love, receiving each person as whole, beloved children of God, radically reframing how human longings, losses, and limitations should be addressed. To Sinek's point, "why" is a crucial question that all spiritual entrepreneurs must answer – but it is the wrong place for innovative ministry to begin. Ministry starts with Who - the God who loves us, and those whom God sends us to love.

Starting with "why" assumes that humans are motivated by reason and reasons. Sinek's view assumes that if we *understand* someone's purpose, we will be *persuaded* to join them. Sure, on some days, this works. But on other days, our actions betray us. I understand *why* I should exercise; sadly, I'm still not motivated to do very much of it. Sometimes I donate to a good cause, and sometimes I don't feel like it. I feed myself instead of my neighbor, especially if she rubs me the wrong way.

These actions demonstrate the truth behind human behavior: we make our decisions in our guts, and *then* we rationalize them with our minds. The word *emotion* comes from the Latin *movere*, "to move" (also the root of the word "motivate"). What we *do* – buy an iPhone, join a cause, come to church, choose a side – has more to do with what we feel than what we think.

And because emotions take place in bodies, they are physiological: when emotions run high, our heart pumps more blood, our respiration increases, our liver puts extra sugar into our bloodstream, we start to sweat.[3] In short, unlike the cool thought processes of the rational mind, emotions prepare our bodies to *act*. The purpose may give our actions direction, but what *motivates* us to take action is arousal.[4]

For those of us interested in mobilizing communities, there is yet another layer to the human motivation puzzle. You don't have to look very far in studies of human behavior to learn that we don't buy a product for what it *does (what)*, we buy it because (we think) it helps us become who we want to be. Even in Sinek's most moving example, Martin Luther King's 1963 "I Have a Dream" speech, King doesn't explain *why* civil rights is a good idea. Instead, he appeals to his listeners' hopes for *who* they want to be. (As Sinek points out, King gave an "I Have a Dream" speech, not an "I Have a Plan" speech). King's genius lay in painting a vision for an alternative future in which oppressed people flourish:

> *I have a dream that one day this nation will rise up and live out the true meaning of its creed: "We hold these truths to be self-evident, that all men are created equal." I have a dream that one day on the red hills of Georgia, the sons of former slaves and*

3   See Ian Burkett, "Social Relationships and Emotions," *Sociology* 31 (February 1997), 37.

4   This, in fact, is how emotions got a "bad name" in the West. The dualistic West distrusted the unruly nature of physiological arousal, in religion as in romance. Theologians from Aquinas to Calvin and Wesley were openly suspicious of using emotion as a gauge for God, given the "fickle" nature of human passions. After all, Christians are called to love others whether we feel like it or not. Even in our century, religious traditions that practice overt emotional display (for example, Pentecostalism) have historically struggled for academic credibility beside their less demonstrative theological cousins. See Bonnie Miller-McLemore, "Coming to Our Senses: Feeling and Knowledge in Theology and Ministry," *Pastoral Psychology* 63 (2014), 689-704.

*the sons of former slave owners will be able to sit
down together at the table of brotherhood. ...I have a
dream that my four little children will one day live in
a nation where they will not be judged by the color of
their skin but by the content of their character. I have
a dream today!*

King did not explain *why* justice mattered; he
illustrated it, describing a nation in which his listeners
became the humans they were meant to be. Their *why*
came from their *who*.

King didn't draw upon marketing advice to make
this point; he drew upon Christian tradition. His
vision of flourishing in a world of justice and hope
materialized from the pages of Scripture, a vision
embodied by Jesus of Nazareth. Christian theology
radically focuses on *Who,* not just why; indeed, our
"why" is unintelligible apart from Jesus, whose way of
being human in the world so radically departed from
the expectations of Empire that the Empire crucified
him for it.

If Apple's objective had been to build a better phone,
it would be a very different company. They might
have succeeded, but it's hard to imagine that they
would have generated much hype. But (despite Sinek's
interpretation), Apple engineers took a different tack:
they asked *who* questions. Who are the people we are
creating this product for? (Apple never targeted the
masses, aiming instead for a high-end, tech-savvy
market.) What kind of lives do they dream of? Steve
Jobs was convinced people wanted the connections
that new technologies made possible, but that people
also yearned for simplicity. He famously badgered
engineers to make their prototypes easier to use.
What if every new technology converged in your hand,

and you could manage it with one thumb? What if the connections we crave – connections with other people (with phones), to information (with the internet), to memories (with photographs), to stories that move us (with movies and music), to technologies that make our lives easier (with calculators and apps) – were as simple as…well, as using our phones?

Purpose matters in ministry – a great deal. It's just that people matter more. In the end, Apple created a device that facilitated human connection to one another and to our world. The energy around the development of the iPhone was not driven by purpose (their purpose was clear enough: capitalize on the iPod's success to ward off competitors who were also developing cell phones). The energy came from Jobs' desire to give people a new kind of experience: being connected to a world we could hold in our hands. We bought it – figuratively and literally. The experience of ubiquitous connection became so deeply tied to human experience that we quickly considered this an extension of ourselves, a surrogate even for face-to-face conversation. Without our connection-makers, we felt lonely and diminished. In very short order, we could not imagine existence without our new artificial limb, permanently tucked in our pocket, and the connections it made possible. Our connection-maker had become part of our "who."

Oh – and it happened to be a phone.

One of the things hampering 21st-century congregations – which have become obsessed with their many shortcomings – has been our insistence on asking, "How can we build a better church?" That is the wrong question. The real question is, "Are we the people Christ calls us to be?" – human beings in communion with God and one another. Our model – and indeed, our power-source – for such a compassion-driven, grace-drenched version of humanity is Jesus. Our vocation always involves becoming more profoundly like Jesus, divinely wired and earthly-born, made from mud but bound for heaven, one with God and one with all the world. We are not called to build better churches. We are called to be better at being human, better reflections of God's love, formed in communities of people stumbling toward Jesus, squinting in the dazzling sunlight of new life.

Christian Social Innovation: Innovating for Love

Today's explosion of interest in innovation has splintered it into many versions. I am primarily interested in a form of innovation that has that has a number of clunky monikers: spiritual entrepreneurship, redemptive entrepreneurship, or the one I'll use, "Christian social innovation." All of these terms refer to innovating for love – but a specific kind of love: it is an effort to embody Christ's self-giving love intentionally, provisionally, and sustainably, in ways that in ways that add value to people's lives, and give them a glimpse of their belovedness and sacred worth.[5] Like the phrase "social innovation" itself, Christian social innovation is a contested phrase, with critics and champions in equal proportion. The debate includes other contested terms as well: social enterprise, social entrepreneurship,

---

[5]   This definition is intended to 1) locate Christian social innovation in theologically informed action; 2) be unambiguously outwardly focused; 3) acknowledge the "trial and error" nature of innovation (and ministry) by claiming its provisional nature; and 4) privilege divine initiative. My definition is influenced by many others. Cf. James A. Phills, Jr., *et al.,* "Rediscovering Social Innovation," *Stanford Social Innovation Review* 6 (2008), https://www.gsb.stanford.edu/faculty-research/publications/rediscovering-social-innovation (accessed July 7, 2021); L. Gregory Jones: *Christian Social Innovation: Renewing Wesleyan Witness* (Nashville: Abingdon), 2016; Scott Cormode, *The Innovative Church* (Grand Rapids: Baker Academic, 2020), 20.

and economic theology, to name a few. I include all of these under the social innovation umbrella.[6] I have not attempted an academically precise definition in this book; my intent is to invite a wide-ranging conversation that welcomes all sorts of humanizing activity – economic, social, existential, spirituall – as part of the work of Christian social innovation.

For Christians, what all of this humanizing work has at its core is an ethic of love, that form of radical, willing self-giving that is patterned after the life, death, and resurrection of Jesus Christ. This is distinctive among definitions of social enterprise – and significant. As Mark Sampson points out, some definitions posit social enterprise as a way to modify capitalism, while other definitions portray it as a way to modify charity. Both camps see social enterprise as a way to heal *existing* systems rather than as offering something new.[7]

But when social innovation is viewed merely as a corrective to existing systems – whether that system is the economy or the church – we lose track of the *social* purpose of social innovation. A third approach (favored by Sampson, and by me) highlights the social aspect of social enterprise and innovation.[8] This perspective focuses less on *what* we do (innovate) than on *Who/who* this work is

---

[6] The line between social innovation and social entrepreneurship is thin, but social innovation is the umbrella category. Since the social entrepreneur's primary objective is not to make a profit, the terms are often used interchangeably. See Sarah A. Soule *et al.*, "Defining Social Innovation," https://www.gsb.stanford.edu/faculty-research/centers-initiatives/csi/defining-social-innovation. Also see Adam Hayes, "What is a Social Entrepreneur?" *Investopedia* (January 18, 2021), https://www.investopedia.com/terms/s/social-entrepreneur (accessed April 22, 2021). The simple definition cited is used by *The Changemaker Initiative*, a ministry profiled in chapter 2. See https://thechangemakerinitiative.org/faq-3 (accessed April 18, 2021).

[7] Sampson's book *The Promise of Social Enterprise: A Theological Exploration of Faithful Economic Practice* (Eugene, OR: Cascade, 2021) is a must-read for anyone interested in the role of theology in social innovation and economic practice.

[8] Sampson lays out this perspective with glittering clarity. See "The Promise of Social Enterprise," 44ff.

for (God and neighbor). It imagines human not just as creatures motivated by survival or self-interest, but as relational creatures, made for friendship with each other, with the environment, and with God.[9]

Making social innovation a practice of self-giving love allows us to bear witness to the divine *Who* in a number of ways. First and most obviously, it makes the life, death and resurrection of Jesus Christ the "plumb line" by which we assess how faithful we are to our goal. If Jesus' love is the template for Christian social innovation, then the measure of innovative ministry cannot be our "great ideas," but the degree to which we embody the lavish, unconditional, last-shall-be-first grace of God.

Second, the phrase *Christian social innovation* sets some parameters on what counts as faithful innovation, which helps us clarify our "yes's" and "no's." Not every instance of social innovation is an expression of faith; as Episcopal Bishop Michael Curry put it, "If it doesn't look like Jesus of Nazareth, you can't call it Christian."[10] For example, if Christ's love is our template, new ideas for institutional survival are ruled out, while new forms of neighboring are ruled in. Changing the church carpet is ruled out, while design that facilitates better human connection is ruled in. Innovating for love is *intentional, provisional,* and *sustainable*. We might stumble upon a great idea by accident but using it to address people's pain and passion takes planning and creativity (*intentional*).

---

[9] This theological anthropology is shared, in some form, by most of the world's religions. Cf. Domenec Mele and Cesar Gonzales Canton, "Views of the Human Being in Religions and Philosophies," in *Human Foundations of Management,* IESE Business Collection (London: Palgrave MacMillan, 2014), 66-87, https://doi.org/10.1057/9781137462619_5 (accessed July 7, 2021).

[10] Michael Curry, interview with Joy Reid, "AMJoy Show," *MSNBC* (June 16, 2018).

Likewise, innovating for love requires humility, *provisional* in the sense that our best effort to love another person, at least until we learn a better way (and then we pivot and try again).

Finally, innovating for love seeks to be *sustainable* by relying more on God's steam than our own. Love requires durable solutions; it allows relationships to lay claim to us, and attending to the financial, physical, relational, and spiritual resources that help love last. Chief among these resources is the innovator's own well-being. A shocking 72% of entrepreneurs struggle with mental illness (primarily depression and anxiety) and one in three entrepreneurs deal with multiple mental health conditions.[11]

Anyone who has ever launched a new idea, especially a "passion project," knows the risk of burnout that comes with it. Only God ignites the bush that burns but is not consumed – which means that faithful innovators have a resource often overlooked in other sectors: grace. We don't have to do it all. Sometimes if we turn aside, we notice a bush on fire: God offering us direction and energy and companions from unexpected sources. Innovating for love means chasing God's vision for creation rather than ours, which requires us to hold our

---

[11] This is far above the national average of adults (one in five) who struggle with various forms of mental illness. Cf. Michael Freeman, *et al.*, "Are Entrepreneurs Touched by Fire?," pre-publication manuscript summarizing research on mental health and entrepreneurs (2015); https://michaelafreemanmd.com/Research_files/Are%20Entrepreneurs%20Touched%20with%20Fire%20(pre-pub%20n)%204-17-15.pdf; David Brown, "Every Entrepreneur Should Prioritize This Risk in 2018, *Inc.* newsletter (January 5, 2018), https://www.inc.com/david-brown/32-percent-of-entrepreneurs-struggle-with-mental-health-prioritize-your-personal-health-in-2018.html; also see National Alliance on Mental Illness, "Mental Health by the Numbers," https://www.nami.org/mhstats. Statistics are from 2019. (All sources accessed July 11, 2021). Despite common associations between mental illness and heightened creativity, evidence connecting the two is scarce. Cf. James Kaufman, *Creativity and Mental Illness* (Cambridge: Cambridge University Press), 2014; also this review of the literature: Charlotte Waddell, "Creativity and Mental Illness: Is There a Link?" *The Canadian Journal of Psychiatry* (March 1, 1998), https://doi.org/10.1177/070674379804300206 (accessed July 11, 2021).

ideas for ministry loosely, giving the Holy Spirit room to rearrange our plans lest we drive ourselves (or others) into the ground. Love eclipses our need to succeed. Innovative ministries may flop, mutate, adapt, change, or fall away. But love never fails.

We've Been Here Before

Perhaps this is obvious, but just in case: understanding Christian social innovation as I am outlining it assumes a fluid understanding of words like *church* and *congregation*. We are moving beyond a single story of what constitutes church, especially in an era when the home and broader community also serve as primary sites for ministry, and not just church buildings. As six-year-olds, we learned in Sunday school that "the church is not the building" – but nearly everything we do in ministry says otherwise.[12] We "go" to church. Our faith community has an address. We meet "at" or "in" a church building. Of course, at one point in our history, having "sacred" space dedicated to nothing but worship was itself an innovation – but one that soon calcified the *ekklesia* (Greek for "gathering" or "assembly") into an organization, often draining it of its spiritual dynamism.

Christian social innovation assumes that church *happens* as well as it exists as an organizational entity, and that congregations occur wherever Christians congregate. Innovating for love evokes "instances" of the church – sometimes around a dinner table, sometimes around a blacksmith's anvil,

---

[12] For a provocative treatment of this problem, see Tim Soerens, *Everywhere You Look: Discovering the Church Right Where You Are* (Westmont, IL: Intervarsity Press), 2020.

and sometimes around an altar. Church happens when people congregate around Christ, regardless of space: wherever two or three are gathered in his name, Christ is in our midst (Matt. 18:20).[13]

This is well-traveled territory for Christians. Historically, before twentieth-century technology co-opted the term "innovation" for itself, people simply pointed to Christian social innovation for the common good and said: "There's the church." Early Christians were known for such ministries. Even during Roman persecutions, Christians continued to give to city benevolences (indeed, this is one way the tiny Christian sect caught the authorities' attention).[14] The Emperor Julian (331-363) saw Christians' invention of social welfare as a major impediment to reviving the pagan religions of Rome. He complained that the Christian faith was especially advanced in "loving service rendered to strangers" and care for the burial of the dead. "It is a scandal," seethed Julian, "that the godless Galileans care not only for their own poor, but for ours as well; while those that belong to us look in vain for help that we should render them."[15]

After the fall of the Roman Empire, innovation was

---

[13] I am distinguishing church (the Body of Christ) from acts of worship. No one instance of church substitutes for the whole, which I take to be all people who participate in the Body of Christ, in all instances, including worship.

[14] When the Roman church sent substantial financial aid to the struggling church in Corinth, the Corinthian bishop Dionysios wrote back: "From the beginning this has been a custom for you, always acting as a benefactor to siblings in various ways, and sending financial support to many assemblies in every city, thus relieving the need of those in want and supplying additional help to the siblings who are in the mines." Paul's letters admonishing churches to remember the poor are an early indication that not all donations were intended for church members exclusively. See Cavan Concannon, "What Early Christian Communities Can Tell Us about Giving Financial Aid at a time of Crises," *The Conversation* (March 30, 2020). https://theconversation.com/what-early-christian-communities-tell-us-about-giving-financial-aid-at-a-time-of-crises-134730 (accessed May 1, 2021).

[15] The fourth century historian Eusebius, cited by Timothy Byerley, *The Great Commission: Models of Evangelization in American Catholicism* (New York/Mahwah, NJ: Paulist Press, 2008), 108.

assumed to be the work of the church, "incubated and entirely powered by the Silicon Valley of the day: monasteries."[16] Medieval historian Lynn White, Jr. demonstrated how medieval monastic agricultural innovations (the heavy plow, the nailed horseshoe, three-field crop rotation) caused an agricultural revolution in Europe that fended off the cycles of starvation that had weakened the Roman Empire. Plentiful food fueled a population boom, which led to economic, cultural, artistic, and technological innovations (including the modern university) – which in turn led to educational and social advancements yielding higher wages and more time for leisure and moral reflection. (This last point, White believed, helped end slavery in Western Europe, between the ninth and thirteenth centuries.)[17] Pointing to Catholicism specifically, Pascal-Emmanuel Gobry proclaimed:

> *Historically speaking, the church has produced countless innovations, both social and technological. It did so prolifically, unabashedly, naturally, relentlessly. More than any particular invention – social welfare, the hospital, the university, the post-slavery economy – what stands out is the mind-set that made it all possible.... Moreover, [that] mind-set was crucial, central to performing the church's work of feeding the hungry, instructing the ignorant,*

---

16   Pascal-Emmanuel Gobry, "The Catholic Church Used to Be Like Silicon Valley. Can It Be Again?" *America* (December 13, 2017), https://www.americamagazine.org/arts-culture/2017/12/13/catholic-church-used-be-silicon-valley-can-it-be-again (accessed July 7, 2021).

17   Originally offered in 1962, White's thesis has recently been re-evaluated (positively) by historians; cf. William Graessle, "Lynn White Jr.'s Medieval Heavy Plow: An Instrument of Agricultural Innovation, Population Growth, and Urbanization in High Medieval Western Europe," *Footnotes: A Journal of History 2* (2018), 27-59. White also blamed the church for our current ecological crisis.

and effecting broad-based social change. And how else should it be? The Bible screams it at us. The Bible is bookended by a narrative of creation and redemption.... That the Catholic Church should put Silicon Valley – or any other institution or culture – to shame when it comes to world-changing innovation is not some tantalizing yet naive prospect. It should be the baseline expectation for any educated Catholic.[18]

Of course, he could be writing for Protestants as well. The Reformation took the innovative spirit of the monasteries and applied it to civic life; Luther's reinterpretation of Scripture around work (for both clergy and laity) effectively created a new structure for public society, and the entire sixteenth century saw numerous new civic experiments address social problems.[19]

This book, therefore, argues that Christians must enact a distinctive approach to social innovation. In short, we are called to participate in God's dream, rather than invoke God's blessing for our own. Christian social innovation sets out to participate in God's redemption of the world in ways that embody the self-giving love of God's signature innovation – the Incarnation, when God took human form in Jesus Christ. In any given moment, God's "new thing" (Isaiah 43:19) is both utterly beyond us and absolutely for us. Inevitably, God's "new thing" disorients us. Without exception, God's "new thing" is an act of divine love, and a manifestation of divine power, revealing who we are as humans and who God is as the author of new life.

---

[18] Gobry, *ibid.*

[19] Hans-Christoph Rublack, "Martin Luther and the Urban Social Experience," *The Sixteenth Century Journal* 16 (Spring 1985), 15; Robert Kingdon, "Social Welfare in Calvin's Geneva," *The American Historical Review* 76 (February 1971), 50.

The Church's Role in New Life

There is no ambiguity about the role of the church as witness to this new life: God calls Christians to participate, not just as bystanders, but as agents deployed by God to share in Christ's liberating, life-giving work. In John 11, Jesus weeps when he arrives at the tomb of his dear friend Lazarus, who was laid to rest four days earlier. "See how he loved him?" the crowd whispers as they observe this tender moment. This is how the life-giving work of the Holy Spirit always begins: in love, not some abstract, generalized sentiment but the deeply particular, personal love of real friendship. Love is the origin of a divine innovation, just as it is the origin of ours.

It is out of love that God does something genuinely new and unprecedented: Jesus calls Lazarus out of his tomb, raising him from the dead. Then Jesus turns to the church – the people in the crowd who have witnessed God's life-giving power – and gives them a job to do: "Unbind him, and let him go."[20] Untie him, let him loose, set him free. Quite literally, the witnesses' job in this story is to remove the strips of burial cloth that are causing Lazarus to trip on his way out of the tomb as he stumbles into the light of day. In other words, Jesus is telling us (the church) to remove whatever binds people to death, whatever makes them stumble, whatever

---

[20] You might justly object that I am using the word "innovation" instead of the more common term "transformation" (distinguishing them credibly goes beyond the scope of this book). I draw on James Loder's work for my understanding of transformation; see *Educational Ministry in the Logic of the Spirit* (Eugene, OR: Wipf and Stock, 2018). For the current discussion, I assume innovation is a fruit of God's transforming grace, with transformation being the larger category, and that the term "innovation" highlights the new life God makes possible in various ways. In human hands, Christian "newness" always stands on the shoulders of God's prior work, as interpreted through Christian tradition, which is what I mean by "traditioned" innovation.

prevents them from flourishing in the new life God offers them. God does the raising; we mop up.

Thus, the task of Christian social innovators is the task of every believer: to unbind one another. The *why* of God's "new thing" is both obvious (love) and secondary to *Who* God's "new thing" reveals (the risen Christ, Love Incarnate). The whole Easter event was so stunningly disorienting that the early church had no words to explain *what* had happened. People could only say *Who* they saw, and again and again, the story was the same: Jesus who was dead now lives. This was the news from the garden, on the road, by the lake, at the table, in the Upper Room. First Jesus died, and now he is *with us*. First, he was dead, and now he is *here*. First, he was crucified, and now he walks *among us*. There was no statement of purpose, only a description of Who they saw, until eventually they could only call this "new thing" that God had done in Jesus Christ a resurrection. Jesus will not let the church – the witnesses to God's "new thing" – approach Easter as bystanders. In the garden after the resurrection, Jesus instructed Mary to "Go and tell" (John 20:17). And when she does, her news is not about *why*, but about *Who*: "I have seen the Lord!" (John 20:18)

We are not called to build a better church. We are called to go and tell about the one *Who* is doing a "new thing." God becomes human, death becomes life – it doesn't get any more innovative than that. The Bible both begins and ends with stories of God innovating, and records God's delight in it. God walks with God's creatures (Gen. 3:8) and invites the cosmos to behold the "new thing" God is doing (Rev. 21:5). Our task as Christian social innovators (in past centuries we would simply have been called Christians) is to untangle people from the grave clothes that are preventing them from living the life God intends for them. We are not building back better. We are not improving church. We have seen the Lord: he has called us from our tombs, and we are unbinding one another as we stumble towards the light.

Oh – and we happen to be a church.

Why Innovation is the Wrong Word

Full disclosure: I hate the word *innovation* (though I'm at a loss for a better one – so I use it, warily, throughout this book). It is one of those terms used so promiscuously today that it seems to mean everything and nothing, which drains it of substance and makes it an easy plaything for every trend that lays claim to it.[21] In the church, we are prone to thinking about innovation as using a really "cool" bucket to bail water out of a sinking ship. It looks like an amazing solution. But two buckets in, we realize that this kind of innovation is not only exhausting; it is futile.

For the sake of this book, I'll start with sociologists' definition of *innovation*, to mean "change that adds value."[22] As noted earlier, social innovation can be many things; but adding the word "Christian" to social innovation suddenly calls for humility. As we will see, Christian social innovation is never novelty for its own sake. Christians are bound to the creativity of God, whether God is making a universe out of love, entering

---

[21] Michael O'Bryan, "Innovation: The Most Important and Overused Word in America," *Wired* (2018), https://www.wired.com/insights/2013/11/innovation-the-most-important-and-over-used-word-in-america/. On various uses of the term "innovation," see https://scottberkun.com/2008/stop-saying-innovation-heres-why/ (both accessed December 11, 2019).

[22] *Open Online Sociology Dictionary,* https://sociologydictionary.org/innovation/#:~:text=An%20innovation%20is%20a%20change,an%20invention%20creates%20or%20discovers (accessed March 8, 2021).

the world as a human, or overcoming death on a cross. Divine innovations are revelations, unmasking God's presence in our world. We can hardly improve on them; we are irrevocably part of them. To be the church is to point to and participate in them as God uses them to smuggle hope, reconciliation, and new life into the world.

The truth is that *innovation* is the wrong word for our impulse to find new forms of ministry and new ways of being the church. The word we are groping for is *love:* How can we love people well given this new context in which we find ourselves? Innovation is the by-product of love, for God and for us. We are never more imaginative than when we are in love, finding new ways to delight our beloved; we are never more creative than when trying to address our children's suffering. Every parent knows that creating solutions for a struggling child is a litany of trial and error – but love won't let us stop until the tears do. As we will see in Chapter Three, love is the relentless driver of Christian social innovation – yet, like the term *innovation* itself, *love* has become such a toothless, squishy word in our culture that it makes people squirm just to say it out loud.

Yet God's radical, surprising, life-giving love is the best illustration of what innovating for love makes possible: devastation becomes hope, deserts become meadows, death becomes resurrection. Divine innovation enacts *agape*, that upside-down, table-turning, sacrificial love that turns Good Friday into Easter. True love may begin as a willingness to suffer for the beloved (every teenager will tell you that true love is "to die for") but it ends in resurrection: it jolts dry bones awake, makes depleted soil bloom, restores shattered communities, and brings hope to dispirited disciples. At Pentecost, the Holy Spirit transforms Jesus' disciples from a bunch of depressed, bumbling peasants into divine envoys, deploying them to every town and village with the good news that death is no match for an innovative God.

This kind of love only seems "innovative" to us because it is rare. We treat those who embody it as anomalies and saints: Francis of Assisi, Harriet Tubman, Florence Nightingale, Oskar Schindler, Dietrich Bonhoeffer, Rosa Parks, Martin Luther King, Nelson Mandela, Mother Theresa. Their love brought changes that "added value" to people's lives, but they did not refer to themselves as "innovators" – they referred to themselves as *Christians*. Both historically and theologically, they were exactly right.

Getting Our Bearings

This book rests on four assumptions that will orient us. The first is that the church desperately needs innovation, understood as actions that express God's life-giving, self-giving love, which is a gift that feels genuinely new to people immersed in a culture where self-serving "love" rules the day. To say that churches need to innovate does not compromise the essential place of Christian tradition; in fact, as we will see, innovation is baked into Christian tradition because love is the back bone of the Christian story. The passages and practices that have conveyed this story for centuries serve as portals through which we glimpse divine innovation at work.[23] It is action that both remembers what God has done and anticipates what God has promised: "Christ has died, Christ has risen, Christ will come again."

---

[23] Cf. L. Gregory Jones and Andrew P. Hogue, *Navigating the Future: Traditioned Innovation for Wilder Seas* (Nashville: Abingdon Press), 2021.

The second assumption builds on the first: Christians need a *theological* understanding of innovation. God does not call us to have "great ideas" – God calls us to have great *love*. No "great idea" outstrips the power of an ordinary idea executed with extraordinary love. Innovating for love must be seen as participating in God's creativity rather than as the fruit of human ingenuity. For Christians, innovation is *inspired* (from the Latin *spiritus*, or spirit): it originates beyond us, in the Holy Spirit who works through us to give shape to God's imagination in the world. Understanding Christian social innovation as a vehicle for love prevents us from falling into the trap of idolizing newness, and it clearly forbids any exploitative or dehumanizing practice. Divine creativity practices resurrection: where new life erupts against all odds, we can be sure God is at work, raising the dead. Our job, like John the Baptist's, is to remove the barriers that get in the way, to make mountains low and rough places plain so that Jesus may travel among us unimpeded. Ministry that does anything less just rearranges the furniture.

The third assumption is that people of faith who take part in social innovation must navigate some rocky shoals carefully. Veer too far in one direction and we'll head straight into the Cliffs of Bigger-Stronger-Faster, which promise that "if we do church right" we can save it, or others, or maybe ourselves – forgetting, obviously, who is the Savior and who is not. Veer too far in the other direction, and we'll be stuck in the Mudflats of Moralistic Therapeutic Deism – convinced that if we "do good things" and help people "feel happy" through social innovation, it's basically the same as following Jesus.[24]

---

[24] Moralistic therapeutic deism, a term coined by sociologists Christian Smith and Melinda Denton in 2009 in the findings from the longitudinal National Study of Youth and Religion, is the

It's not. That confusion is only possible because American Christianity's systems of faith formation are in tatters, causing many people, even in congregations, to confuse Christianity with other things we value, like optimism, hard work, charity, patriotism and friendliness. Those values have their place, but they aren't "Christian values" in the sense that they help us follow Jesus (in fact, they often get in the way). The interrelated institutions – families, churches, educational systems, etc. – that once helped people wrestle with God's story in multiple contexts, at multiple stages in our lives, have largely disintegrated as contributors to faith formation. Sociologists Christian Smith and Amy Adamczyk argue provocatively that, due to multiple shifts in our culture, the family (biological or *de facto*) is now the *only* institution capable of genuinely forming faith – if it is formed at all.[25]

As a result, people who want to follow Jesus often only know the tip of the iceberg of the story they are part of, which makes it hard to pick out God in a crowd. It surprises people, for instance, to learn that Jesus said a great deal about compassion but nothing at all about "being nice," or that he never advocated "feeling happy." (People in the United States have higher expectations for happiness than anyone in the world, and feeling happy was not a cultural priority until the 1800s. Even Thomas Jefferson called for the pursuit – not the

---

belief that religion is useful to the extent that it helps you be nice and feel good about yourself, but otherwise God stays out of your way. The NSYR found MTD to be the dominant religious outlook among youth and parents in the United States. No research since the NSYR has refuted this. See Christian Smith and Melinda Denton, *Soul Searching: The Religious and Spiritual Lives of American Teenagers* (Oxford and New York: Oxford University Press), 2009.

25 Christian Smith and Amy Adamczyk, *Handing Down the Faith: How Parents Pass Their Religion on to the Next Generation* (Oxford and New York: Oxford University Press), 2021.

feeling – of happiness).[26] Jesus' idea of happiness meant flourishing (*eudaimonia*), which is a state of knowing you are beloved and blessed, something closer to joy. In the ancient world, *eudaimonia* was a communal good. My ability to flourish depended on whether you were flourishing too. For Jesus, the route to such flourishing is *love* – self-giving, not self-fulfilling, love – the kind that willingly sacrifices so that others may live. When Jesus took on death and resurrection, he wasn't "doing a good thing." He was demonstrating divine love, which for Jesus meant you lay down your life for your friends.

To be sure, this power-through-weakness approach to love and flourishing was a supremely innovative move on God's part – but it's not usually where our minds go when congregations start talking about Christian social innovation. It is quite difficult for most of us to recognize Christ's footprints in the world, and to distinguish them from ours. Our best chance may be to view social innovation through the lens of *vocation* – as work that helps us discern God's calling in our lives, and that helps us use our gifts creatively to reflect Christ's light for others. Approached vocationally, social innovation *can* powerfully shape disciples; in fact, it might be one of the most powerful faith-builders available to contemporary churches. Many examples are offered in the insets throughout this book. But just because social innovation is motivated by the right things does not mean it forms faith. Nor can we assume that social innovators have learned about God elsewhere and are "applying" their faith through social innovation. For social innovation to inspire, inform,

---

[26] One historian linked the emergence of happiness as a cultural value with improvements in dentistry. Cf. Peter Stearnes, "The History of Happiness," *Harvard Business Review* (January-February 2012), https://hbr.org/2012/01/the-history-of-happiness (accessed July 25, 2021).

and deepen our faith requires explicit attention to *Who* we follow, and ongoing, prayerful effort to distinguish God's work from our own.

One final assumption stands behind this project. I believe that, despite our quick dismissal of churches as stubborn institutions resisting new things, most congregations really do want to innovate, now more than ever. We sense new possibilities for following Christ in this work. As we will see, innovation requires more than someone with an idea or "a person with a plan." Innovation requires a culture, an ecology of support and some concrete, teachable tools. That means that congregations must begin to understand themselves as incubators of ongoing innovation, making it a normal part of their daily work. When people look for the most creative voices in their community, for the souls most committed to making their neighborhood into a crucible for human flourishing, a congregation should be the first place people look. I do not mean to suggest that churches or ministry communities enact innovative love alone. On the contrary, church leaders need to reclaim their historic roles as "conveners of creativity" for their communities, inviting stakeholders from multiple backgrounds, cultures, and professions, to "take captive every thought" for Christ (2 Cor. 2:5) in order to eradicate suffering, sow delight and smuggle peace into their neighborhoods. Christian leaders are not always called to *be* innovators, but they must claim responsibility for inspiring, equipping and blessing this work in others.[27]

---

[27] I am grateful to the Rev. Kathleen McShane, founder of the Changemaker Church Movement, for elucidating the role of the pastor in this work; I turn to her approach to the role of the pastor as the one called to "inspire, equip, and bless" spirtual entrepreneurs repeatedly through this book.

A Christian vision of human flourishing requires ministry communities to discern what to do in a given situation and to have the practical *chutzpah* to respond in ways that allow people to see themselves as beloved and blessed.[28] This is the heart of what Hebrew Bible scholar Walter Brueggemann calls a "prophetic imagination."[29] This imagination is the spiritual gift of every Christian social innovator. God sends every disciple as Jesus was sent – in human form, to concrete communities, as bearers of God's grace and good news, heralds of the life God has imagined for us. Christian social innovation creates paths for this good news to travel, loosening one another's grave clothes as we go.

As you move through the pages of this book, you will see my own attempts to wrestle with these four assumptions. In Chapter Two, we will explore why Christians innovate. Chapter Three situates Christian social innovation theologically and historically; just as NASA indirectly gave us inventions like memory foam and dust busters, Christian communities over the centuries have indirectly offered countless social innovations – "life hacks" – that helped people to thrive, especially the poor.[30] Chapter Four offers some guidance for faith communities hoping to begin this prophetic journey. In the conclusion, Chapter Five, I offer some

[28] The connections between practical theology and design thinking and, specifically, the importance of prototyping are too obvious to ignore, but they are beyond the scope of this book. See especially the emerging work of younger practical theologians like Amanda Hontz Drury at Indiana Wesleyan University, Beth Ludlum at Wesley Theological Seminary, Mark Sampson at Rooted Good, Victoria White at Leadership Education/Duke Divinity School, and Andrew Zirschky at Austin Theological Seminary.

[29] Cf. Walter Brueggemann, *The Prophetic Imagination, 40th Anniversary Edition* (Minneapolis: Fortress), 2018.

[30] Josie Green, "Inventions We Use Today Were Actually Created for Space Exploration," *USA Today* (July 8, 2019), https://www.usatoday.com/story/money/2019/07/08/space-race-inventions-we-use-every-day-were-created-for-space-exploration/39580591/ (accessed April 25, 2021).

personal reflections on why this approach to ministry gives me hope – and some of my lingering doubts. In order to stretch our imaginations, each chapter includes snapshots of innovative ministries in the insets, and discussion questions at the end. And if you're really motivated, you'll find 10 exercises in the Appendix to help your group or Expedition Team get started.

Three Hopes

You could argue that churches do not need to innovate – being part of the Body of Christ is innovation enough (unaccustomed as we are to practicing resurrection, this inevitably feels radical and new). But because God gives us a clear role to play in God's life-giving work, innovating for love enacts a prophetic imagination by liberating people from the entanglements that prevent them from flourishing. Since other books show *how* churches can innovate (or at least how to begin some imaginative processes), I'm taking a run at *why* people who follow Jesus innovate. Our task as the Church, in this and every era, is to become the witnesses God made us be: the body of Christ, people who practice self-giving love and participate in resurrection. Compared to the self-preserving, death-dealing, soul-crushing ways many people get through an average Tuesday, self-giving love is a "new thing" indeed.

So let me leave you with three hopes. First, I hope this conversation helps you and your ministry community view participating in God's innovative love as the church's default setting, not as an extracurricular activity you might get around to when you're not so tired. This kind of ministry – let's call it what it is – is prophetic work, so it is central to our calling as

Christians. Not only is the twenty-first century church uniquely positioned to do such ministry; the strange new shores on which we find ourselves as a culture shaped by COVID-19 give us new ears to hear the cries of those we have been slow to address in the past.

Second, I hope you will come away convinced that *aiming* for innovation is the wrong way to score. Innovation follows mission, not vice versa; Christians do our best innovating indirectly, when we pay more attention to the needs and longings of the people in our neighborhoods than to our "great ideas," so that we can become stakeholders and not merely service providers in our communities. Theological indirection is a lost art for many ministry communities, but it is one that our culture desperately needs Christians to reclaim.

Third, I hope you will see this moment as a time of unprecedented opportunity for the church and claim your place in it. Precisely because some versions of church are no longer viable or desirable, new possibilities are emerging that combine old traditions and practices in new ways, allowing us to redesign and nurture genuinely post-Christendom ministry communities. Not since the Reformation has so much energy gone into discerning what it looks like to be Christ's body in the world. If you leave these pages feeling a little bolder, a little lighter, a little more ready to risk making your life look more like Jesus' – you are already innovating, redeeming the wreckage for the next leg of your journey toward God.

Conversations

- Share about a time you got tied up in grave clothes. What stopped you from living from living the new life Jesus wanted for you?

- What part of God's dream for your community would you most like to see come true?

What Next?

- Identify the place on the Innovation Journey (p. 139) that best describes where your group or Expedition Team is right now. If your team is very early in the innovation process, exercises 2-4 (readiness to innovate [p. 141], the importance of connection [p. 144], and the design process [p. 147]) will help you get your sea legs.

CHAPTER TWO

So This Is Malta:
The Good News of Shipwreck

"People who believe in the resurrection, in God making a whole new world in which everything will be set right at last, are unstoppably motivated to work for that new world in the present."

N.T. Wright, *Surprised by Hope*[1]

"This is not the crisis. This is the time before the crisis."

Pastor surveyed during the COVID-19 pandemic (April 2020)[2]

Captain Joynal Abedin had navigated rough water before, but never like this. After four months at sea, Abedin and his crew were waiting for authorization to "sign off" (to get their salaries and go home) when the sudden tropical cyclone – the kind Mediterranean sailors have feared since ancient times – pinned them offshore of Malta. "As we realized the wind was picking up," Abedin told the *Times of Malta*, referring to the violent storm that engulfed the island on February 10, 2018, "I asked

---

[1]   N.T. Wright, *Surprised by Hope: Rethinking Heaven, the Resurrection, and the Mission of the Church* (San Francisco, CA: HarperOne, 2008), 214.

[2]   Andrew MacDonald et al., "Survey: How Churches Are Responding to the Coronavirus Crisis," *Outreach Magazine* (April 1, 2020), https://outreachmagazine.com/resources/research-and-trends/53889-survey-how-churches-are-responding-to-the-coronavirus-crisis.html (accessed May 9, 2021).

Maltese authorities for permission to seek shelter closer to shore." Permission granted, Abedin started the engine to steer his crew and their 885-ton bunkering vessel inland. In mere minutes the ship crashed into Malta's craggy shoals, sending captain, crew, and contents flying. They escaped with their lives – and were quickly cared for by locals bearing blankets, food, and clothing.[3]

If the story sounds familiar, there is a reason. In better weather, February 10 is a festival in Malta – the Feast of St. Paul's Shipwreck, to be exact, when the streets of the capital are festooned with eye-popping garlands and brilliantly dyed banners. The day begins with a mass at The Parish Church of St. Paul's Shipwreck, which claims to possess the relics of St. Paul's right wrist bone and a piece of the column on which he was beheaded in Rome. After mass, a procession carries a statue of St. Paul through the streets, accompanied by marching bands, fireworks and endless streams of confetti flung over the parade route by children hanging from windows and balconies.

All this is to commemorate another shipwreck in Malta, not far from where Abedin's vessel ran aground. In 60 C.E., so the story goes, another Mediterranean storm threatened a ship sailing from Turkey, filled with grain and prisoners bound for Rome. One of the prisoners – the apostle Paul – had warned his captors back at port that such a late-season voyage was ill-advised. (In his speech delivered during the tempest, he can't resist a quick "I told you so"). Yet throughout the ordeal, Paul encouraged his fellow shipmates to take heart, for the God he served had assured him that none would be lost.

---

[3]   Sarah Carabott, *Times Malta* (February 12, 2018), https://timesofmalta.com/articles/view/captain-of-ship-which-ran-aground-on-sunday-describes-ordeal.670452 (accessed February 28, 2021).

Sure enough, as the ship broke apart in the raging storm, all 267 people onboard miraculously made it to shore by swimming or clinging to pieces of the ship. Washed up on a shore they did not recognize, Paul and his bedraggled, bone-soaked shipmates were immediately welcomed and warmed by the natives (Acts 27:1-28:11).

The apostle Paul is the patron saint of Malta. As Acts tells it, the locals inform the shivering men of their whereabouts and offer Paul and his shipmates both fire and friendship. Paul spent three months on Malta, where he astonished people with his apparent immunity to venomous snakes (he shook a viper off his hand on his first night onshore) and his gift for healing (he cured many people of diseases, including the father of the local governor). Interestingly, Acts records no conversions in Malta, but it is clear that Paul and his companions shared the gospel there and won the Maltese's trust and affection. When spring came, they gave Paul all the provisions he needed to continue his fated journey to Rome (Acts 28:1-11).

Knee-Deep in Flotsam: Why Shipwreck Is Good News

For most of the world, the year 2020 was a shipwreck-of-a-year like no other. The COVID-19 pandemic claimed more than five million souls worldwide. America's overt racism was captured on camera in the murder of George Floyd, a black man, by a white police officer, unleashing a hurricane of protests, demands for reform and some real soul-searching as many Americans wrestled with their complicity in such events. The pandemic pried open already-untenable income gaps, predatory economic practices and disparities in health care and education. Climate change gnawed at our shorelines, detonated wildfires and stoked menacing storms with relentless frequency. And then, as if the year needed a fitting

31

Genesis: The Floating Church

Hackney Wick, London

The 2012 Olympic Games in London transformed Hackney Wick – once the gritty site of slaughterhouses and wrecking yards – into a hipster paradise alongside a towpath lined with longboats, microbreweries, vegan restaurants, and canoe rentals. Yet, in the young adults moving in and out of the tech startups and warehouse apartments that now define Olympic Park, the Rev. Dave Pilkington saw something else. He saw longing. "I love the Olympic Park," he told The Guardian in an interview on October 19, 2020:

> ...but for a lot of local people, it felt like this stuff had been foisted on them. There was a sense that people were being pushed out, that all these new facilities weren't for them. In an area undergoing such drastic transformation, with a whole new community arriving, we were wondering what role the church could play. Where was the space for spirituality in the midst of such rapid change?

The answer was Genesis, a "bobbing place of worship," established by the entrepreneurial Diocese of London (Church of England), which had already created housing initiatives, therapy centers, gyms, and cafes on church lands across the diocese.

Genesis is a small architectural wonder: it is built on a barge with a pleated roof that rises and falls so it can float under London's bridges. It seats 40 for worship in its community-friendly chapel on board and is – literally – designed to go wherever people need it. Genesis will be moored in Hackney Wick for five years, working with two local parishes to build up a local congregation called St. Columba (after the Irish missionary-evangelist whose voyages are credited with spreading Christianity to Scotland). Genesis will then "set sail" for another similarly changing neighborhood along London's waterways. "Rather than investing millions in a new building," says Pilkington, "you can take the boat in and see what grows out of that, then look to establish something."

finale, on January 6, 2021, extremists staged a deadly attack on the United States Capitol, attempting to stop the certification of Joseph Biden as the newly elected president of the United States.

It was as if the two evil eels from Disney's *The Little Mermaid* – the Sea Witch's diabolical henchman who create mayhem in every scene – had morphed into the Kraken and unleashed destruction on a global scale. The eels' names, appropriately, are "Flotsam" and "Jetsam," and they personify havoc and ruin. Flotsam and jetsam are a ship's wreckage, debris hurled toward shore like broken bath toys, pitched by one angry wave after another. Technically, jetsam is the cargo thrown overboard to lighten the ship; flotsam refers to the broken parts of the vessel itself that are claimed by the sea. And yet, in Acts, flotsam is also the stuff of salvation. As Paul's ship disintegrates, Acts tells us, those who could swim jumped overboard and made for land – and the rest followed on planks or pieces of the ship. "And so it was that all were brought safely to land." (Acts 27:44)

The story of Paul's shipwreck on Malta is, surprisingly, a story of hope. For one thing, despite devastating destruction, no one drowns. That's good news for many churches that were already taking on water before 2020. One in three practicing Christians stopped attending church altogether during the pandemic, and early reports suggest that many are not coming back.[4] The Lake Institute, which tracks churches' financial health, estimated in 2020 that almost 40% of American churches lacked the cash to

---

[4]   In the summer of 2021, after most communities in the U.S. had re-opened following the coronavirus crisis, congregations reported a 12% drop in attendance (combined online and in-person worship attendance). Attendance at in-person events and services dropped more dramatically. Scott Thumma, "Exploring the Pandemic Impact on Congregations," Hartford International University for Religion and Peace (November 10, 2021).

Also see Cooperman, "Will the Coronavirus Permanently Convert In-Person Worshippers to Online Streamers? They Don't Think So," *Pew Research Center* (August 17, 2020), https://www.pewresearch.org/fact-tank/2020/08/17/will-the-coronavirus-permanently-convert-in-person-worshippers-to-online-streamers-they-dont-think-so/ (accessed March 7, 2021); "One in Three Practicing Christians Has Stopped Attending Church in Covid-19," *State of the Church 2020* (July 8, 2020), https://www.barna.com/research/new-sunday-morning-part-2/ (accessed March 7, 2021).

GoFish! Ministries
Pullman, Washington

In 2016, the congregation was struggling, membership aging, and budgets dwindling. The Rev. Matt McNelly, the youth pastor of Pullman Presbyterian Church (where his wife Amy was the head of staff) voluntarily cut back his hours.

The problem was, as the parents of four children, the McNelly's had to offset Matt's salary cut. That was when McNelly found a state-supported fishing program that paid up to $8 per fish for anglers to catch Northern Pikeminnows, a species threatening the salmon population in the Snake River.

McNelly's first thought was that he had found the perfect summer job. As an avid outdoorsman, the idea of fishing all summer – for pay – seemed too good to be true. Then he got an idea. He began investing in fishing equipment, lifejackets, and (thanks to a gift from an enthusiastic parishioner) a 24-foot pontoon boat. That's when he invited the middle high youth of Pullman to *GoFish!*

Today, each June McNelly and his interns take groups of pre-teens (those too young to have "real jobs," McNelly explained) out on the Snake River for daylong fishing expeditions, overnight trips, weeklong fishing camps or multi-night fishing excursions. McNelly gives them a 360 in creation care: youth are up at dawn to dig bait, and every day they deal with the elements, and each other, on the boat. Spiritual practices like prayer, silence, communal meals, readings and discussions punctuate the fishing (as McNelly told me in an email, "There is no shortage of Bible stories about fishing you can tell on a boat.")

GoFish's program fees are nominal, and many young people make a profit on their catches at the end of the day. But they also experience hard work, and failure is real. McNelly considers confronting failure an important spiritual practice (and life skill) for youth to experience. Even the disciples had days they failed as a fisherman – a feeling McNelly identifies with (from his email: "I'm still waiting for Jesus to show me 153 fish...") After his first summer on the boat, he confided: "I have never been this tired in my whole life...or had this much fun!"

To McNelly, each trip is a spiritual journey. He likens *GoFish!* to a floating monastic community, where young people pray and work together, and grow spiritually through cooperation and beholding the beauty of creation. "I want kids to experience the wildness of the world," he says, "and to understand that in the midst of that creation, God speaks."

last more than three months. One 2020 report predicted that one in five churches (one in three mainline ones) would fold within eighteen months.[5]

For the most part, these statistics simply laid bare already-familiar trends in American religious life; most social observers agree that the pandemic did not cause institutional crises as much as it accelerated those already underway. The pandemic essentially drop-kicked American Christianity 20 years into the future, with no time to either prepare or argue. Some saw it as an apocalypse, not in the sense that the pandemic was the end of the world, but in the way it exposed hidden fault lines: the Greek *apokalupsis* means "uncovering" or "revealing."

As a result, an odd thing happened. Churches that long resisted change suddenly found themselves – without much protest – trying something new. The danger, of course, was assuming that innovation was a temporary response. What became devastatingly clear as the multiple debacles of 2020 unfolded was that upheaval, and the innovation it inspired, had become our "new normal." As one prescient church leader observed: "This is not the crisis. This is the time *before* the crisis."[6]

To be clear, the Church itself was not, and is not, in jeopardy. But Jesus' promise that the church will prevail (Matthew 16:18) should not be construed as a promise of eternal life for every expression of the church, much less

---

[5] "The Virus Is Accelerating De-Churching in America," *The Economist* (May 23, 2020), https://www.economist.com/united-states/2020/05/23/the-virus-is-accelerating-dechurching-in-america (accessed March 6, 2021). A United Church of Christ study predicted church closures of two to three times the normal rate following the pandemic (Richard Reinhard, "Redeveloping Houses of Worship," *Center for Analytics, Research and Data* [April 1, 2021], https://icma.org/articles/pm-magazine/redeveloping-houses-worship (accessed September 19, 2021).

[6] Andrew MacDonald *et al.*, "Survey: How Churches Are Responding to the Covid Crisis," *Outreach Magazine* (April 1, 2020), https://outreachmagazine.com/resources/research-and-trends/53889-survey-how-churches-are-responding-to-the-coronavirus-crisis.html (acceessed April 24, 2021).

for Christendom. Like all human creations, religious institutions emerge from particular moments in history, and come and go accordingly. Indeed, even before 2020, many faithful Christians had begun to ask themselves: "How much of the church as we know it are we willing to let go of in order to follow Jesus?"

It is clear today that certain religious outlooks flying under the banner of "Christianity" should be abandoned. Even in mainstream churches, much of America's religious rhetoric echoes the Declaration of Independence, Emerson's *Self-Reliance,* and even political platforms more than the teachings of Jesus. We are all prone to fashioning the gods we can live with instead of following the God who chose to live with us. Humans create the gods we can stomach – gods who share our tastes and values, biases and ambitions. When "good Christian people" invoke Christ's name while instigating unthinkable evil, we rightly recoil and wonder, "What kind of God would sanction such a thing?" The answer is: the gods we have fashioned in our own image, who approve the evils we like best.[7]

So we should probably celebrate the success of our current ecclesial "rummage sale" – Phyllis Tickle's memorable term for historical periods, popping up every 500 years or so, in which the church unloads some of its accumulated baggage, throwing overboard structures and ideologies that create a drag on the church's mission.[8] Inevitably we accidentally jettison

[7] I have written about this in "Stranger Things: Reclaiming the Oddness of Jesus in Youth Ministry," *5 Views on the Future of Youth Ministry,* ed. Mark Oestreicher (San Diego: Youth Cartel) 2021. Thanks to Pastor Harland Redmond, whose sermon on Phillippians 3:7-14 articulated these ideas better than I could, and whose phrasing I have adapted here (Kingston United Methodist Church, Jan. 10, 2021).

[8] See Phyllis Tickle, *The Great Emergence: How Christianity is Changing and Why* (Grand Rapids: Baker), 10`1.

some good with the bad, but one of the miracles of Christianity is that we reliably survive downsizing, and even thrive as lighter vessels with fewer organizational entanglements. What's more, as Paul's shipwreck in Acts demonstrates, the flotsam from a broken church may also be the lumber God is giving us to rebuild, to reimagine, and to repurpose our boat, augmented with local materials and expertise from our new context.

This is the second reason the shipwreck of Acts 27 is good news. Early Christians conceived of a ship as a symbol of the church, an "ark of salvation." Since a ship's mast and yard form the shape of a cross, when persecution made it dangerous to speak of the church, believers instead referred to a *navis* ("ship" in Latin, the root of our word *nave*). In many ways, the analogy still holds. Riffing on H. Richard Niebuhr's metaphor of "shipwreck" for an existential loss of meaning, Sharon Daloz Parks describes the experience of shipwreck as "the coming apart of what has been a shelter and protection, and has held and carried one where one wanted to go, the collapse of a structure that once promised trustworthiness."[9] A devastating illness, a deflating failure, a disastrous moral choice, a searing disappointment or betrayal, a loss of job or relationship or purpose – all of these storms can capsize us. Losing a significant faith community that once protected and legitimized some of our most cherished relationships and ideals can feel similar. "It's almost like a death in the family," observed a church council member of St. Casimir's Church in Lansing, Michigan, a 99-year-old congregation that

---

[9]   Sharon Daloz Parks, *Big Questions, Worthy Dreams* (Hoboken, NJ: Wiley and Sons), 24.

came to a swift end during 2020's lockdowns.[10]

Yet in Parks' view, what matters is not that our boat goes under but that we can situate this loss under a larger canopy of significance – a master narrative that acknowledges death but is not undone by it. Shipwrecks happen to individuals and to churches. The question is, what happens next? Parks sees two possible narratives to choose from. In one story, we drown. In the other, we wash up on a new shore where there is gladness, amazement and a sense of vitality.[11]

Saved by Malta: The Call to Innovate

The church is neither dying nor presumed dead. But we have been transported to a coastline we don't recognize, where surprising gladness and even new life await us. The strangers we meet here find us as strange as we do them. For centuries now, we have designed church to serve Christendom: we have treated Christian communities as pillars of the broader culture and erected buildings and cultivated outlooks and habits that have often been indistinguishable from the Empire around us. No wonder so many people today consider Christian faith expendable. If it fails to offer an alternative to the reality we already know, why bother?

By contrast – thanks in part to events of 2020 – those of us in the 21st century church find ourselves on a very different landscape, where church is being reimagined on different terms. People are hammering away at a new kind of church in grottos and crevices, rather than on hills and town squares. These builders are "nones"

---

[10] "The Virus Is Accelerating Dechurching in America" (May 23, 2020), https://www.economist.com/united-states/2020/05/23/the-virus-is-accelerating-dechurching-in-america (accessed March 7, 2021).

[11] Parks, 43.

and nonbelievers, devoted Christians and the formerly
faithful, nominal believers and the newly curious, people
ousted from the "old church" and those who never missed
a Sunday, "spiritual entrepreneurs" and twitchy youth,
eager to make a difference. This new vessel is smaller,
lighter and more missionally agile than our previous ark
of salvation. Indeed, post-pandemic congregations *are*
more like boats than buildings – less apt to be destinations
than dinghies transporting pilgrims and prisoners
alike to the next port seeking hope. Their destination is
Christ, not us. Those of us who commit to this voyage as
Christians sign on as the ship's crew, not its passengers.
We are the people at the oars. Christ is at the helm.

If one virtue stands out in this COVID-shaped
church,[12] it is humility. On this new island, churches
are de-centered, which allows God's voice to be heard
on different frequencies, and by different ears. This
new church is not made for Christendom; it is cobbled
together from the pieces of Christian traditions and
practices that have come ashore with us, which are
being rewoven with materials native to this moment and
place in history. All pretense of cultural influence has
been lost at sea; our confidence in our "call to convince"
has been shaken. What people on Malta seem curious
about isn't our universal truth, but our individual
stories of how God saved us and brought us to shore. It
is a disorienting place for churches to stand; we still feel
a little lost. But it is also oddly liberating. Christ has
turned the tables: in this place, holy curiosity matters
more than excellence; being kind is more important
than being right; discerning Jesus' path is as necessary
as declaring it.

---

[12] Thanks to Rev. Eddie Rester for this language, which acknowledges the continued disruption
to life and identity caused by the global pandemic.

Conetoe Family Life Center
Conetoe, North Carolina

Every chance we get, my colleague Nate Stucky and I take our class to Conetoe, North Carolina, to plant cabbages with the Rev. Richard Joyner. Joyner was named a 2015 CNN Hero for revolutionizing health in his community. Like many in Conetoe, Joyner hates farming. Like some of his parishioners, Joyner was the son of a sharecropper. He grew up watching his father tend crops from dawn till dusk, only to receive nothing at the harvest. After so many stolen harvests, Joyner's generation grew up vowing to do anything with their lives – except farm.

When Joyner became the pastor of Conetoe Chapel Missionary Baptist Church, Edgecombe County ranked 97/100 counties in the state for health and socio-economic well-being. Shortly after Joyner arrived, emergency medical services (EMS) made 200 trips to Conetoe in a single year – for a population of just 300 people. Thirty people died that year, mostly young, mostly from preventable, diet-related diseases. Joyner remembers driving home after preaching at a young father's funeral. "I just couldn't look another child in the eye who just lost her daddy and tell her everything was going to be alright – because that was a damn lie." Wracked with grief, he pulled over to the side of the road to pray: "Lord, what do you want me to do?"

As Joyner tells it, when he opened his eyes, he looked around and saw nothing but fields. "I said, 'Is there anybody else up there?'" But he knew he had his answer. He had to bring fresh food to Conetoe, and that meant farming.

His congregation fought the idea – this was a step back toward sharecropping. But the youth in the church convinced their elders to give it a try. Tobias Hopkins, 17, started working in the garden because two uncles and a cousin, all under age 50, died of strokes. Tationa Hymana, 8, came after her father died of complications from high blood pressure, diabetes, and dialysis.

Teenagers dug and 10-year-olds planted. Joyner had a nutritionist come to church monthly and preached health as part of Jesus' hope for their community. As crops came in, youth proudly took home beans, squash, cabbage, tomatoes, lettuce, peppers, onions, and okra. For a season, Conetoe feasted on fresh vegetables.

That year, the number of EMS trips to Conetoe dropped to *three*. The local hospital was so shocked that they called Joyner to see what was going on. It turned out that the pastor had started a garden with some kids.

Worship is central to life in Conetoe; on most Sundays, Joyner preaches in his work clothes. But the heart of his ministry is Isaiah 11:6, "A little child shall lead them." Youth negotiate every contract. They contact store owners and stock the shelves. They learn the business of running a farm, gaining real-life experience in science, math, and financial planning. They know that they have made a life-and-death difference in their community. Joyner believes that changing children through education and opportunity equals change for the whole family.

Today, the Conetoe Family Life Center grows 50,000 pounds of produce each year – enough for everyone who works to take home as many vegetables as they can carry. They sell the rest at a farm stand, to the local hospital and to the Piggly Wiggly supermarket, thus improving health and incomes at the same time. The CFLC offers nutritional counseling, after-school programs, summer camps, cooking classes, wellness programs, and a very successful beekeeping business (the youth took a vote about the bees; Joyner, who was opposed to it, got outvoted). Beekeeping was Tationa's idea. At age 8, she became the youngest certified beekeeper in the state of North Carolina. "You have a whole community willing to grow itself out of poverty," Joyner said. "This is as spiritual as it gets."

This is Malta. Had 2020 not completely blown us off course, we might never have come here. Many churches might have continued their slow slide into becoming "zombie institutions" – sociologists' term for institutions that continue to exist long after they stop serving a purpose.13 Instead – in spite of ourselves – we are very much alive. We would have far preferred for Malta to find us, so we would not have needed to leave our cozy beds. But here we are in Plan B, tired and wet and exposed, learning from strangers. On unfamiliar terrain, we must improvise. Innovation is no longer an extracurricular activity for churches that can "afford" it. We are all innovators now: on Malta, innovation is the work of the church. Bringing "the rich resources of the Christian tradition to bear on the mindsets, practices, and traits of social innovation"14 is less of an activity than a landscape we have moved into as we discern where the Holy Spirit is leading us next. Paul may have been the reason Christianity took root on Malta, but make no mistake: God used Malta to save Paul. Malta was as important to Paul's salvation as vice versa – which begs the question: What if God has disoriented the 21st-century church for a reason? What if God is using Malta to save us?

What Makes Christian Social Innovation Different?

On the surface, Christian social innovation might seem indistinguishable from its commercial or social cousins – but there are crucial distinctions. If Christian social innovation means joining in God's "new thing" rather than roping Jesus into ours, then

---

[13] Coined by sociologist Ulrich Beck, "zombie categories" have been used by many sectors. Cf. Elizabeth Sepper, "Zombie Religious Institutions," *Northwestern University Law Review* 112 (March 2018), https://scholarlycommons.law.northwestern.edu/nulr/vol112/iss5/1/ (accessed March 7, 2021).

[14] See L. Gregory Jones, *Christian Social Innovation: Renewing Wesleyan Witness* (Nashville: Abingdon Press, 2016). Jones borrows from Gregory Dees' 1998 definition of social innovation, as work that: 1) adopts a mission to create and sustain social value; 2) recognizes and relentlessly pursues new opportunities to serve that mission; 3) engages in a process of continuous innovation, adaptation, and learning; 4) acts boldly without being limited by the current resources at hand; and 5) exhibits heightened accountability to the constituents served and for the outcomes created (pp. 2-3).

its most distinguishing characteristic is *humility*. We are participating, at Christ's invitation, in redemption that God already has well underway; this "new thing" is energized by Christ's resurrection, not by our abundant enthusiasm or passionate commitment (or stubbornness). When we innovate for love, we do not run on our own steam.

This is as true for institutions as for individuals. In fact, participating in God's innovation requires the church's humility as well. The church is only one of God's chosen instruments; if we don't join in God's "new thing," God certainly has other options. Humility raises the possibility that churches may no longer be the tip of the spear when it comes to addressing the world's pain. But congregations can notice and name what God is doing through others – maybe even through other faiths – and come alongside these spiritual entrepreneurs with alternative visions of truth, theories of change, additional resources and a toolkit full of spiritual practices.

Ask four spiritual entrepreneurs what makes "spiritual" innovation different from any other kind – and you'll get ten different answers. But a recent retreat with the Changemaker Church Movement in Los Altos, California did exactly that.[15] The movement's convener, the Rev. Kathleen McShane, noted that most of us live happily disintegrated lives; it is far easier to compartmentalize the dissonant parts of our fragmented existence than to integrate them into a whole. Yet for McShane, this is exactly the blessing of Christian social innovation (her word is

[15] I have paraphrased these conversations; phrases that are mostly verbatim have been placed in quotation marks or block quotes. Kathleen McShane, Daniel Pryfogle, Elan Babchuck, and Kenda Creasy Dean, panel discussion, Changemaker Church Movement Opening Retreat Panel, Los Altos United Methodist Church (Los Altos, CA), May 1, 2021.

"changemaking"): it brings our compartmentalized lives together, banishes the Sunday-Monday divide, and prevents faith from being tacked on at the end. Changemaking creatively unifies life in the neighborhood with life as a disciple, guided by actions we undertake in the service of Jesus Christ. McShane is also convinced that changemaking is a lay movement: "God is using laypeople's ministries, as much as pastors, to invest in the future God wants in this world. That's when I can put the world into their hands instead of thinking I have to hold it all in mine."

In the same panel, Rabbi Elan Babchuck, founder and director of the Glean Network, which supports spiritual entrepreneurs of all faiths, distinguished different forms of innovation in terms of impact. "Social innovation has to have social impact, commercial innovation has to have commercial impact," observed Babchuck:

> So spiritual entrepreneurship in some way [should help] people should feel more deeply aligned with the divine, more deeply reminded that they were created in the image of God, and therefore have infinite value.... By participating in spiritual entrepreneurship, do people act differently at the Y the next day? Do they hesitate a second longer before categorizing people or judging them?...It's not a bottom line metric...But if the desire is there, if it is planted by God, it is work that we cannot not do.

Panelist Daniel Pryfogle, co-founder and CEO of Sympara, a community that repurposes religious assets for the common good, added that spiritual entrepreneurs have a different motivation than other social entrepreneurs: "We are invited to participate in something already underway – God is already doing this new thing, jump on board!" Pryfogle thinks the role of ego sets spiritual entrepreneurship apart. "[Secular] social innovation is framed as a heroic endeavor," says Pryfogle. "We get all sorts of ego rewards – change the world, make things better. In the heroic framework, everything starts with the hero." The expectation that "it all depends on you" leads us to burn both ends of the candle and stay up late, fueled by a fearful drivenness. But in Christian social innovation, there are other forces at work that relieve our anxiety. Pryfogle says:

> *We have a different understanding of power ("'by my Spirit,' says the Lord of hosts"). We have an invitation to participate in divine power, who plants in us a yearning to create. But the framework is different; it is not a heroic endeavor. It's grounded in a community, not ego.*

To be sure, there's another version of this; the flip side of the hero-preneur is the martyr. When our plans to heroically save the day go sour, we play the victim. (Quipped Pryfogle: "It's kind of the fun and the not-so-fun sides of narcissism.") He offered the story of Elijah as Exhibit A. Exhausted from escaping Jezebel's murderous rage, holed up alone in a cave in the middle of nowhere, Elijah laments (whines?) to God: "I am the only one left!" (I Kings 19:10)

God's response is tender. In the story, God treats Elijah as a human, not a hero. First: here, eat a little something. Then: I am here. And finally: reassurance. No, Elijah, you're not the only one left. God, as it turns out, has lots of friends in the city – 7,000 to be exact. So, God seems to be saying to Elijah, go back. And then God gives him the name of someone who can run the next lap. On God's list of helpers in the city was the young farmer Elisha, who carried Elijah's ministry forward.

The Burden of Innovation

Of course, one of the first signs that we are running on our own steam instead of God's is the fact that our steam runs out. During the quarantines of the spring of 2020, most congregations in the United States underwent instant and nearly unimaginable transformation. Within weeks, innovation moved from the fringes of Christian life to its center. Heated arguments about the potential gains and losses of internet ministries were cast aside in a nearly unanimous pivot to online worship services that church leaders could offer their traumatized flocks. Many leaders found themselves pastoring people they had never met, who sometimes lived in different states, but who found real solace and sustenance in their new online church family. Online attendance decreased among "regulars" but, at the same time, online services suddenly made church accessible for neurodiverse persons, people who struggle with mobility, and others who found in-person participation difficult. The fact that Holy Week was less than a month after the shutdowns presented another conundrum: what about sacraments, whose physicality seemed to require in-person participation? Again, most congregations traded purity for pragmatism: some wondered aloud if the Holy Spirit's gift of grace through the internet was any weirder, when you think about it, than God using material objects like water and bread and wine in-person?

Those early, grueling days of the COVID-19 quarantines made one thing clear: for all its blessings, innovation can be exhausting. Drawing on our own resources for the constant pivots that the early pandemic required sapped our creativity and drained our spirits. Leaders quickly burned out from "innovating," with little to show for it.

In reality, almost all this early activity was adaptation, not innovation, as congregations tweaked their usual offerings for the new online environment. Yet these adaptations did help us become more familiar with our new landscape, which seemed to require a different kind of imagination than the ones we had honed during centuries of Christendom. On this new land, no one speaks our religious language, cares about our influence, knows about our polity, or identifies with our piety. Like Dorothy after the cyclone – or like Paul's shipmates after the storm – the only thing we can say with confidence is that we're not in Kansas anymore. And so we find ourselves taking our first tentative steps on a road we have never traveled, to a destination we cannot yet see.

It is important to realize that the kind of innovation needed on Malta goes far beyond the noisy "worship wars" of the 1980s, the experimental "emerging church" of the 1990s, or the self-replicating multi-site church campuses of the 2000s. Today's conversation is not about how we "do" church when we gather; it's about whether we gather in the first place, and whether any congregation's particular way of being church matters to anyone besides ourselves.

One of the benefits of being washed up on an unknown island is that it forces us to re-think our operating metaphors – habits of thinking that make us undecipherable to people who don't use them. Yet changing our metaphors feels quite risky. What if people stop thinking of church as a building we go to, and start imagining it as a way of being embedded in a community that follows Jesus?[16] What if "mission" no longer means expanding the church's "reach," but

---

[16] See Tim Soerens, *Everywhere You Look: Discovering the Church Right Where You Are* (Westmont, IL: Intervarsity Press), 2020.

committing to a neighborhood where our Christian witness shows more than it tells? What if "practicing faith" means we don't have it right yet – and Christian life is more of a rehearsal than a performance? What if "practicing resurrection" became as probable in pubs as in pews?

If you are reading this book, these kinds of questions already haunt you; your metaphors for church are probably already shifting. You got to Malta early and have likely already explored some new possibilities for ministry in this context (*see insets*). You have taken to heart 50 years of research describing religion's accelerating loss of traction with North Americans, especially with young people. You already know how exhausting, uncreative, and unsatisfying it is to reduce innovation to modes of acquisition – i.e., getting more "butts, buildings, and budgets." You may have already begun to wonder what it looks like when Christian communities flourish, not because they are strategic or even potentially successful, but because they add sacred value to human life.

The truth is, innovating for love is often maddeningly *un*strategic, since our goal is to imitate Christ, not preserve systems. Christian innovators are often tediously *un*successful, since the only way to discover the balm that works on a bee sting is through trial and error. Christian social innovators meddle in multiple disciplines and look for divine footprints in the sand as well as by the altar. The result is that innovating for love is often clunky, not excellent; provisional, not permanent; self-giving more than self-enhancing. It carries risk – financial, structural and moral. People who start innovative ministries are typically less concerned with whether the ship breaks apart than

Growing Change
Wagram, North Carolina

Noran Sanford, a United Methodist social worker and mental health therapist in Wagram, North Carolina, did not plan to live out his faith in this way. After years of work in social services, Sanford attended the funeral of one of his middle school clients who had been killed in a gang incident. Sanford said: "I had to be honest with myself that the system had not done everything it could do, that I had not done everything I could do." So, he began to pray – and suddenly he began to notice the decaying Scotland Correctional Facility that he drove by each day going to work. The Scotland Correctional Facility was *actually* a zombie institution – still standing, but decommissioned, no longer useful in today's society.

That is when it came to Sanford to "flip" a prison – with teenagers.

Sanford founded *Growing Change* with formerly incarcerated youth to reimagine the future of North Carolina's decommissioned prisons. Sanford was used to working with young people considered "throwaways" by various social systems. Now, he saw a possibility to turn the tables by making them essential personnel and giving them a real decision-making agency. He invited a group of these young people to walk through the Scotland Correctional Facility property with him. When they finished, he handed them the keys. "What can we do with this?" he asked them.

What the youth imagined – and built – was an educational farm created and run by teenagers who have done time (today *Growing Change* also includes teenagers facing additional struggles). They keep bees, rotate a grazing herd of sheep for wool and meat, care for hens, compost waste, tend an organic garden, and more. When I met Sanford in 2017, he had just received plans from M.I.T. to realize another idea generated by *Growing Change*'s youth: turning the prison watch tower into a climbing wall.

Today, formerly incarcerated youth serve as Sanford's board of directors. He appreciates the upside-down power dynamics in this arrangement ("I work for them," he told me). *Growing Change* receives support from multiple community partners, as well as area congregations. But the real leaders of *Growing Change* are the young people, whose leadership of the program restores their sense of worth and confidence as contributors to their communities.

with being able to throw people planks when they get in over their heads.

Only Jesus Christ saves the church. The fact that we can be seduced into thinking that a "big idea" might rescue us merely underscores the burden of innovation. Christians' distinctive take on innovation is that it doesn't start – or end – with us. Only God truly creates *ad novum*, making something genuinely new. And the "new thing" God is doing – bringing new life by shaping worlds out of nothing, healing the sick, giving sight to the blind, raising the dead – is mostly for Malta, not for the people on our boat. This is the *missio dei* that God invites us to share; indeed, God has established the church for this purpose. If we board this "ark of salvation," safe passage is not guaranteed; the waters are choppy, and our current means of navigation are woefully inadequate. Yet we are Christ's body, called to smuggle God's grace into a storm-tossed world (John 20:21). If innovation exhausts us, it is because the storm is fierce, and our imaginations are small. But God has imagined nothing short of our salvation and will stop at nothing less.

From Protest to Panacea: Whiplash and Pendulum Swings

Canadian historian Benoit Godin points out that the term "innovation" has been contested for 2,500 years; only in the 20th century did innovation seem to become "a panacea for every socioeconomic problem."[17] In ancient Greece, "innovation" (from the Greek *kainos*) was considered dangerous, fomenting instability and revolution, whereas in ancient Rome, *innovo* meant "renewal," a refreshing and welcome new beginning.

---

[17] Benoit Godin, *Innovation Contested: The Idea of Innovation Over the Centuries* (Milton Park, Abingdon, Oxfordshire: Routledge, 2015), 8.

The pendulum swung back and forth between meanings until the Protestant Reformation, when the term migrated from politics to religion. Godin calls innovation a powerful concept "that helped enforce the [Protestant] Reformation."[18] Despite the fact that the Reformation was one the most important innovations of the millennium, innovation in 1517 was considered heresy. Both Protestants and Catholics hurled the label at one another.[19] In England in the 1530s, Henry VIII (himself a legendary innovator) instructed his ambassadors that he would not "tolerate" innovation. In 1548, Edward VI issued the first royal injunction against innovation, and declared it punishable by imprisonment "and other grievous punishementes."[20]

By the 1600s, "other grievous punishementes" meant cutting off innovators' ears. In the 1630s, a Puritan cleric named Henry Burton, invoking Proverbs 24:21 (King James version: "My son… meddle not with them that are given to change") accused the Archbishop of Canterbury and his episcopal minions of innovations in church doctrine and discipline, charging them with "popery."[21] Burton was not a master of tact; he called the bishops "caterpillars" and "antichristian mushrumps."[22] The bishops countered that it was

---

[18] Benoit Godin, "Innovation Theology," *Project on the Intellectual History of Innovation* (INRS: Montreal, 2020), 1. http://www.csiic.ca/en/innovation-and-religion/ (accessed April 21, 2021).

[19] Some religious traditions, such as Islam and Eastern Orthodoxy, still maintain a connection between innovation and heresy, though in practice innovation is both common and inevitable in every tradition. See Trine Stauning Willert and Lina Molokotos-Liederman, *Innovation in the Orthodox Christian Tradition?* (Milton Park, Abingdon, Oxfordshire: Routledge), 2012 and Edmund Burke III, *The Ethnographic State: France and the Invention of Moroccan Islam* (Oakland, CA: University of California Press, 2014), 175.

[20] Cited by Godin, "Innovation Theology," 3.

[21] Richard T. Hughes, "Henry Burton: The Making of a Puritan Revolutionary," *Church and State* (1974), 421-434, https://academic.oup.com/jcs/article/16/3/42/856085 (accessed April 21, 2021).

[22] P. Heylyn, *Cyprianus Anglius: or the History of the Life and Death of The Most Reverend and Renowned Prelate William [Laud], Archbishop of Canterbury* (A. Scile: London, 1668), 330.

Burton, the Puritan, who was the innovator, responsible for pulling the Anglican Church into new and "nonconformist" directions. The bishops prevailed, and in 1637 Burton lost his ears and was imprisoned for "seditious preaching."[23] (His wife appealed to Parliament for his freedom; in 1641 the trial was declared illegal, and Burton was released.)

But then, the pendulum began to swing back again. By the 19th century, social reformers reconceptualized innovation as an instrument for progress, not revolt. In the 1800s, socialism, social reform, and social innovation were terms used interchangeably. Whenever churches worked for the common good, such as when Catholicism introduced education for all, they were accused of "social innovation," which was sometimes called the "new Christianism." For the establishment, it was sedition; for the innovators, it was divine calling. As one reformer put it, "The gospel...will always be the guide and the model of the social innovator."[24] It was the 20th century's association of innovation with technological breakthroughs that gave the word its current halo effect. Technology severed innovation from its religious moorings. Indeed, innovation became a kind of modern religion, an ideal and value in itself.[25]

This brings us to the "moment" social innovation currently enjoys in our culture – the panacea

https://play.google.com/books/reader?id=niYX8RfJAvoC&hl=en&pg=GBS.PA1 (accessed April 21, 2021).

[23] Original source material, including biographical material sympathetic to Burton (and graphic in its retelling), are available at *A Puritan's Mind,* "Biography of Henry Burton (1579-1648)," https://www.apuritansmind.com/puritan-favorites/henry-burton-1606-1654/ (accessed April 21, 2021).

[24] Cited in Godin, "Theological Innovation," 5.

[25] Godin, 5.

Godin warned us about. Even today, the pendulum of innovation is not fixed. To some, it is salvation; without it, we are lost ("Innovate or die!"). To others, it is a siren, a seductive decoy – beguiling but fatal to the church's mission because innovation valorizes human potential and accelerates our already frenetic existence.[26]

Despite all the noise, a third way to think about Christian social innovation seems to be emerging, in which innovation is neither God nor mammon. This third way rejects all views of innovation that replace divine inspiration with human ingenuity and shuns novelty for the sake of "progress." But it also maintains that the church is called to notice, name, and participate wherever God unleashes life-giving creativity through practices that add value to human life. To be clear, by "value" I do not mean human value; humans have equal and infinite worth to God, no matter what the shape of our lives. But if we are to live in the world in a way that relieves suffering, adds meaning, and magnifies joy, innovation matters. The impetus for Christian social innovation is not having a great idea, maximizing productivity, or needing to survive. We innovate for love in order to give shape to a prophetic imagination, and to embody a vision for human flourishing patterned after Jesus, whose way of being human is the template for our own.

---

[26] For a theological critique of finance capitalism, see Kathryn Tanner, *Christianity and the New Spirit of Capitalism* (New Haven, CT: Yale University Press), 2019; for the argument that unbridled social acceleration is a characteristic of late modernity, see Stephen Bertman, *Hyperculture: The Cost of Human Speed* (Santa Barbara, CA: Praeger), 1998 and Hartmut Rosa, *Social Acceleration: A New Theory of Modernity* (New York: Columbia University Press), 2015 and *The Future of the New: Artistic Innovation in Times of Social Acceleration* (Amsterdam: Valiz/Antennae), 2019.

Redeeming Our Wreckage

The Great North Pacific Garbage Patch is a floating island of ocean plastic in the Pacific, twice the size of Texas. It serves as a humiliating reminder that we are not thoughtful about our flotsam and jetsam.[27] Examining what we throw overboard is a kind of Rorschach test for what we value – and what we are willing to jettison to save our own necks. In 1973, when the oil tanker Zoe Colocotronis ran aground near Puerto Rico, the captain ordered 1.5 million gallons of crude thrown into the ocean. He lightened the ship enough to deliver its payload – but not without unleashing an "ecological maelstrom" on the region. More sickening still was the cargo ship Zong, which transported 442 enslaved Africans from Accra to Jamaica in 1781. It overshot its destination, adding two weeks to the journey, which taxed the ship's supply of drinking water. The captain therefore ordered the crew to throw 132 slaves – men, women, and children – into the sea; he then collected insurance on the "lost cargo." A well-publicized court case followed, but only because of the insurance claims. Those murdered were simply recorded as lost property – jetsam.[28]

Thankfully, God has a different attitude toward wreckage than we do. What we deem useless, human or material, God calls beloved, infused with holy purpose. In God's hands, everyone gets to shore and even the splintered pieces of tired institutions can be instruments

---

[27] The Great North Pacific Garbage Patch did inspire a computer game that invites players to gather ocean plastic and build a floating city. So there's that. "Flotsam," https://www.pajamal-lama.be/flotsam/ (accessed March 7, 2021).

[28] Kevin McDonnell, *Human Waste and Wasted Humans: Flotsam and Jetsam in the Anthropocene* (July 8, 2019), "The 18th-Century Common," https://www.18thcenturycommon.org/macdonnell/ (accessed March 21, 2021).

of salvation. God uses the very same vessel that sinks Paul to save Paul and his companions. So maybe we should wonder: if this was God's plan for Paul's broken vessel, what does God have in mind for ours?

Conversations

- Name something that has changed in your community. How well has your church or ministry community addressed this change?

- What part of the broken church – what "flotsam" – have you found yourself clinging to in a recent stormy period? How did it bring you to shore?

- When was the last time a problem in the world or in your community wouldn't "leave you alone"? Why did it capture your imagination?

What Next?

- Before your group or Expedition Team takes the plunge to start a new ministry, do the Empathy Conversations on p. 154.

CHAPTER THREE

The Great Loosening: Innovating for Love

"Tell all the Truth but tell it slant."

Emily Dickinson[1]

"Love made me an inventor."

Maggy Barankitse[2]

The last thing Maggy Barankitse planned to be was a social entrepreneur.

When rebels stormed the Catholic bishop's compound in Ruyigi, Burundi where Maggy worked in October 1993, there was no time to flee. On a tip that the bishop was harboring Hutus, the militia broke in with machetes and machine guns. Maggy crammed her seven adopted children into the sacristy cupboards and prayed for their safety. Incredibly, because Maggy was Tutsi, the soldiers did not murder her. Instead, they stripped her naked, tied her to a chair, and forced her

---

[1]   Thomas H. Johnson, ed., *The Complete Poems of Emily Dickinson* (New York: Little, Brown and Company, 1960), 506-507.

[2]   Maggy Barankitse, "Love Made Me an Inventor," *Faith and Leadership video* (September 12, 2011), https://www.youtube.com/watch?v=PWSxAA4nOg0 (accessed March 7, 2021).

to watch them butcher seventy-two people, including Maggy's best friend Juliet. In Juliet's last breath, she asked Maggy to educate her children. Then the soldiers beheaded Juliet and threw her head into Maggy's lap.[3]

When the rebels finally released Maggy, she bribed them to free 25 more children, in addition to her own brood huddled in the cupboards. After that, children kept coming. "I had . . . eighty after a week, and 200 a month later," she remembered. "They needed love, they needed safety, and they needed food and clothing. I simply had to invent ways to help them."[4]

For Maggy, teaching children scarred by genocide to forgive their enemies was as vital as giving them shelter, food, and education. *Maison Shalom* with its mission of forgiveness became home to 47,000 orphaned children over the next 26 years. Maggy organized children into households, where older and younger youth practiced love and forgiveness as "families." Meanwhile, to meet the children's physical needs, Maggy started small businesses – a farm, a mechanic's school, a tailor's shop, a hospital, a hair salon, a mortuary, and an international school, to name a few – which also provided jobs and generated revenue. Determined that children should dream and not just survive, Maggy added a movie theater, and then a swimming pool "because the water of our baptism cleans all the sin." (She located the swimming pool on the killing field where she had seen 72 people slaughtered.) By 2015, *Maison Shalom* was a vibrant

---

[3] For one account of Maggy's story, see L. Gregory Jones, *Christian Social Innovation: Renewing Wesleyan Witness* (Nashville: Abingdon, 2016), 74ff.

[4] Maggy Barankitse, interview, Berkley Center for Religion, Peace, and World Affairs, Georgetown University (October 17, 2011), https://berkleycenter.georgetown.edu/interviews/a-discussion-with-marguerite-barankitse-maison-shalom-burundi (accessed March 28, 2021).

network of schools and training programs, agricultural cooperatives, and more than 3,000 homes across Burundi, galvanized around a mission of forgiveness and care. She shrugs off her talents as a changemaker, saying simply: "Love made me an inventor."[5]

In 2015, it all fell apart.

Once again, genocide split Burundi, and a price was put on Maggy's head. She escaped to Luxembourg posing as a diplomat's wife, but *Maison Shalom* was eviscerated, and its assets confiscated. Eventually, Maggy and her staff found their way to the Rwandan refugee camps, where more than 90,000 Burundian refugees had taken shelter. Half of them were under 16.[6]

Maggy started again.

In Rwanda, *Oasis of Peace* has a familiar entrepreneurial vibe. Like *Maison Shalom*, it gives young people a Christian framework of forgiveness in which to rebuild their lives. As a place "where refugees can feel human again," *Oasis of Peace* provides preschools, primary schools, and high schools, mental health services for victims of torture and rape, and small businesses for vocational training and income.[7] At this writing, Maggy still lives in exile, but whenever she is asked to speak, her message is the same: because she is a Christian, love made her an inventor – and it can make us inventors too.

---

[5] Maggy Barankitse, "Love Made Me an Inventor," video.

[6] Joe Shute, "Why the 'Angel of Burundi' Fears Her Country Is Sliding Back into Genocide," *The Telegraph* (November 25, 2016), https://www.telegraph.co.uk/women/politics/angel-burun-di-fears-country-sliding-back-genocide/ (accessed March 28, 2021).

[7] Maggy also found host families and scholarships for 300 refugee students to attend the University of Lyon in France, until Covid-19 restrictions sent them back to Rwanda. Interview, "16 Days of Activism," Nobel Women's Initiative (n.d.), https://nobelwomensinitiative.org/meet-marguerite-barankitse-burundi/; also, Interview, Aurora Humanitarian Initiative (June 19, 2020), https://auroraprize.com/en/unprepared-worst-danger-covid-19-refugees (accessed March 28, 2021).

The Innovation Bank Shot: Aim for Love

Innovation works like a bank shot in basketball. A bank shot happens when a player shoots for the backboard instead of the rim, so the ball bounces off the backboard into the net. Researchers at North Carolina State University simulated a million basketball shots on a computer and found that a bank shot is 20% more effective than a "swish." As a result, players are often coached *not* to aim for the hoop – but to shoot *past* the hoop for something larger, the backboard.[8] It is less sexy than a swish, but it is a more reliable way to score.

Christian social innovation, like scoring on a bank shot, is best achieved indirectly, when we aim for something bigger. When we aim for *love,* innovation follows. Indirectly, love is innovation's backboard and field of operation. In a sly piece of theological writing, Emily Dickinson advised:

> *Tell all the Truth but tell it slant –*
> *Success in Circuit lies...*
> *The Truth must dazzle gradually*
> *Or every man be blind.*[9]

Let that sink in for a minute. Whether Dickinson intended her Truth to mean Jesus has been debated, but it is a striking description of what theologians call "divine accommodation" – the idea that God's Truth is too dazzling for us to handle in one go.[10] So to avoid

---

[8]   Larry M. Silverberg, et al., "Optimal Targets for the Bank Shot in Men's Basketball," *Journal of Quantitative Analysis in Sports* 7 (2011), https://www.eurekalert.org/pub_releases/2011-03/ncsu-tpo031011.php (accessed April 17, 2021).

[9]   Thomas H. Johnson, ed., *The Complete Poems of Emily Dickinson* (New York: Little, Brown and Company, 1960), 506-507.

[10] See Paul Helm, *John Calvin's Ideas* (Oxford, UK and New York: Oxford University Press, 2006), especially 184-208.

overwhelming us, God goes about divine revelation "circuitously" – indirectly, bit by bit, through a baby in a manger who grew up as the son of a carpenter and became an itinerant teacher given to making points through parables – flummoxing the Jews and generations of scholars trying to make sense of God's bankshot: the divine decision to reveal power indirectly, through weakness.

Theologians like John Calvin interpreted the indirect nature of divine revelation as an act of pure mercy on God's part, since a direct encounter with divinity would be far more than we can withstand. In the Hebrew Scriptures, people hid their faces from the Lord, believing that gazing directly at God's holy light, like staring into an eclipse, would harm them. Yet God desires relationship; so, like a patient lover, God takes things slowly. To protect ancient people from unfiltered divine brilliance, we are told, God visited them indirectly – through dreams and angels, burning bushes and gentle whispers. In the Incarnation, God "accommodated" our limited human capacity by becoming the thing humans relate to best – another human.[11] Limiting God's divine nature, the Almighty wrapped Truth in skin and walked beside us as Jesus. People may have seen divine light shooting out of Jesus' pores, but that's not what they reported; mostly, they reported things that Jesus *did* – halting storms, healing the sick, raising the dead – that suggested something bigger was afoot. God held back, allowing the disciples to discover Christ's divinity along the way: bit by bit, meal by meal, conversation by conversation, miracle by miracle, all the way to the

---

[11] Cf. Stephen Wedgeworth, "Theories of Accommodation in the Theology of John Calvin," *The Calvinist International* (February 15, 2015), https://calvinistinternational.com/2015/02/04/theories-accommodation-theology-john-calvin/ (accessed May 1, 2021).

cross and beyond – knowing, perhaps, as T.S. Eliot put it, that "humankind cannot bear very much reality."[12] For Reformation theologians, all of this was evidence of God's tender care for humanity. God told all the Truth in Jesus Christ, but told it slant.

The Power of Indirection

Catholic educator and practical theologian Thomas Groome tells the story of visiting St. Joseph's Convent School in Karachi, run by the Sisters of Jesus and Mary since 1856 – the crown jewel of Pakistan's 550 Catholic schools. Remarkably, these schools are funded by the government. Fewer than 5% of the students are Christian; Muslim parents vie for their child to get a slot, knowing that there are no symbols of the Christian faith in any school, and that children will receive instruction in their own religious traditions.

Pakistani parents told Groome they wanted their children in Catholic schools because these schools were "different." When he asked how, parents said the Catholic schools promoted the value of the person, emphasized equality between girls and boys, encouraged a positive outlook on life, and challenged the fatalism of the surrounding culture. The schools promoted friendships across ethnic divides, and encouraged students to develop a personal spirituality, to commit to peace and justice, and respect those who are different. St. Joseph's also had a strong academic curriculum that encouraged critical thinking, in contrast to the rote learning methods of government schools.

Groome was intrigued by the fact that St. Joseph's

---

[12] T.S. Eliot, *Four Quartets* (Quartet No. 1), http://www.davidgorman.com/4quartets/ (accessed April 17, 2021).

can teach none of these things catechetically – from the perspective of Christian faith – yet Christian values permeate the school's ethos. "Though we cannot instruct in Christian faith," one sister explained, "we see to it that gospel values pervade the life of the school and the general curriculum." Groome asked the principal if she ever felt their Christian mission was compromised by the mandate to avoid all forms of evangelization. She seemed surprised and responded immediately: "Oh no – to educate well is always to do God's work – that is enough!"[13]

This kind of indirect witness – making our lives, our relationships, and our work on behalf of others in our communities such powerful embodiments of God's redemptive love that they point beyond us – is a lost art in many Christian communities. Yet indirection is deeply embedded in the church's DNA and has occasionally been claimed as the explicit methodology of certain religious communities, especially religious women, whose unconventional roles in public life made them innovators in multiple fields. In 19th-century France, the indefatigable "Daughters of Charity" built and led institutions, staffed medical clinics, and created systems of care for the poor that were replicated worldwide. Their approach to mission was intentionally indirect; "Say little, do much," St. Vincent de Paul allegedly advised them (one wonders if he would have given "sons" of charity the same advice).[14]

Jesus himself was a master of indirection; he rarely

---

[13] Thomas Groome, *Educating for Life: A Spiritual Vision for Every Teacher and Parent* (Allen, TX: Thomas More, 1998), 10-11.

[14] Sioban Nelson, *Say Little, Do Much: Nursing, Nuns, and Hospitals in the Nineteenth Century* (Philadelphia: University of Pennsylvania, 2001), 5, 167. See Chapter 3 for Elizabeth Ann Seton's Sisters of Charity's involvement in free enterprise.

claimed to be God, preferring to let his actions speak. He hinted, he healed, he told parables – not to mention making God present on earth in an entirely new and unexpected way. He relied on his actions to reveal his Messianic identity. For the most part, only after people got curious did he become theologically explicit. Theological conversation was crucial, but it was "insider" language—for dialogue with the faithful who wanted to know more about Jesus.

Ancient Christians followed suit, making their indirect witness as champions of the poor, healers of the sick, creators of art, makers of institutions, and vessels of grace the early church's primary form of Truth-telling outside the context of worship. North African theologian Tertullian, writing at the end of the second century, imagined a day when warring pagans would point to this indirect witness and say of Christians: "See how they love one another!...and how Christians are ready even to die for each another!"[15] A century later, he got his wish; Emperor Julian the Apostate – whom we heard from in the Introduction – was beside himself at being upstaged by a tiny band of Christians:

> *Why do we [pagans] not observe how the kindness of Christians to strangers, their care for the burial of their dead, and the sobriety of their lifestyle has done the most to advance their cause? . . .Do not therefore let others outdo us in good deeds while we ourselves are disgraced by laziness.[16]*

[15] Adapted for readability. Tertullian, *Apologeticus*, in Susan Ratcliffe, ed., *Oxford Essential Quotations*, 4th edition (New York: Oxford University Press, 2016), ch. 39, section 7. https://www.oxfordreference.com/view/10.1093/acref/9780191826719.001.0001/q-oro-ed4-00010813#:~:text-t=Tertullian%20c.ad%20160%E2%80%93c,readier%20to%20kill%20each%20other (accessed April 16, 2021).

[16] Julian the Apostate, *Letter to Arsacius*, around 360 CE, trans. Edward J. Chinnock, *A Few Notes on Julian and a Translation of His Public Letters* (London: David Nutt, 1901) 75-76, as quoted in D. Bren-

Clearly, the "privatization" of faith that Americans take for granted was not on the minds of Christianity's first practitioners. There was no sense that ministry should focus on the faith community itself, though Christians famously cared for one another. Indeed, the *purpose* of the faith community was to worship God and be an example of Christ's love for the sake of people who were *not* part of the church. The thrust of ministry was to ensure that all people would experience God's grace and love, which meant finding creative ways for the *whole* community to flourish, whether or not people "bought in" to the spirituality on offer.

Love Innovates: Mother Bunny Theology

It's worth pointing out: For most of human history, what we call "social innovation" has just been called love. Innovation might sound like it belongs in someone else's wheelhouse but love resoundingly belongs in ours. Love innovates because God does. In another sly theological classic – the 1942 children's book, *The Runaway Bunny* by Margaret Wise Brown (stay with me) – we see this point illustrated perfectly.[17] To refresh your memory: On page one we meet a baby bunny who wants to run away. Instead of stopping him, Mother Bunny simply says: "If you run away, I will come after you." If Baby Bunny becomes a fish, Mother Bunny becomes a fisherman. If Baby Bunny becomes a crocus in a garden, Mother Bunny becomes a gardener. If Baby Bunny becomes a bird, Mother Bunny becomes the

---

dan Nagle and Stanley M. Burstein, *The Ancient World: Readings in Social and Cultural History* (Englewood Cliffs, NJ: Prentice Hall, 1995) 314-315.

[17] Margaret Wise Brown, *The Runaway Bunny* (New York: HarperFestival), 1942. The book first appeared in 1942, the same year the Battle of Midway, Nazi approval of "The Final Solution," and thirteen-year-old Anne Frank's first diary entry; it sold to a warring world in desperate need of assurance – which is exactly what it delivers.

The Changemaker Initiative
Los Altos, California

It was a gamble – but when Los Altos United Methodist Church founded The Changemaker Initiative, its motto was: "Risk something big for something good." What if a church connected the compassion of Jesus with the skills of social innovation? And what if pastors supported lay people in ministries they designed, instead of asking laity to support the ministries of pastors?

Twenty-five "Changemaker Fellows" were selected, ages 12 to 75, for a nine-month fellowship that began by asking each of them: "What do you see in your community, school, workplace, family, or church that is broken or missing or unfair?" Fellows created projects out of their own passions – helping unhoused youth through storytelling, creating jobs for under-resourced teen artists, preventing gun violence, launching an arts center, and creating a teen tech ministry. Some ideas soared, some didn't.

But change happened – partly because Changemaker Fellows were not just driven by their projects. As a result of their work together, they felt compelled to follow Jesus in more concrete ways and to strengthen their connection to their faith and church. Some 80% of participants say they have discovered new ways to talk about their faith, 80% have applied their change-making learning to other parts of their lives, and 50% have taken on significant new leadership roles in their congregation. "In twenty years of ministry, I've never seen a more effective disciple forming experience," says Los Altos UMC pastor Kathleen McShane.

McShane is adamant that changemaking is a lay discipleship movement. Pastors, she says, have three crucial tasks in supporting innovation: inspire it, bless it, and talk about it theologically. In 2020, the church received a $1 million grant to launch a movement of "changemaker churches." Today, the initiative involves congregations from across the U.S., partnerships with multiple organizations, and a network of alumni whose faith has been strengthened by approaching social innovation through the lens of faith. As alumnus Melissa Allison put it, "The Changemaker Initiative has given me a life, and a faith, that I've always wanted."

tree he flies home to. And so it goes, until Baby Bunny finally gets the picture, and Mother Bunny lands her deliciously satisfying closing line: "Have a carrot."

Yes, it's a story written for two-year-olds – but it is

also a stunning portrayal of love's relentless creativity, which in Christian tradition is embodied by a God who insists on loving us, whatever that takes, in spite of our determined efforts to wander off. Maternal love is famously and ferociously inventive, which is exactly how ancient scribes portrayed the love of God. Undeterred by our attempts to run the other way, God meets us with divine ingenuity at every turn so that we will flourish in spite of ourselves. An ark? A fish? A shade plant? A still, small voice? The most prominent image of all is the Good Shepherd, who promises every wayward sheep: "If you run away, I will come and find you." God's love takes whatever shape is necessary to be with us – all the way to human form, all the way to death itself.

God's creative solutions – creation, incarnation, redemption, to name some of the most obvious – are innovative only in retrospect. Their purpose is larger – God's "dream come true," as Father Gregory Boyle puts it: radical kinship, the reconciliation of all creation to God and one another.[18] Innovation, ours and God's, is a bank shot. It is the natural consequence of aiming for the thing behind it: love. Maggy Barankitse did not innovate because she had a great idea, or because she needed a new revenue stream for the church. She did not seek to innovate *at all*. Her sole aim was love – and from love, innovation flowed.

Honey, I Shrunk the Church

Churches' reluctance to innovate stems from our history, not our theology. We've already traced some of this history in the Introduction. For much of the past

---

[18] Gregory Boyle, *Barking to the Choir: The Power of Radical Kinship* (New York: Simon and Schuster, 2018), 4, 165.

2,000 years, religion was no place for an innovator. As society grew more complex, institutions grew more specialized, which further discouraged churches from pioneering solutions for the broader culture. We carved up institutional job descriptions (labeling church activities as "spiritual" and political, social and economic activities as "profane"), which meant we stopped learning from each other's various forms of expertise. Soon churches stopped mingling with secular institutions much at all, and we grew suspicious of one another's motives. Without the ethical constraints of religion, business and politics could (and often did) become unmoored from moral responsibility, and without the community relationships required by business and politics, churches could (and often did) become insular and self-absorbed.

The American colonies have their own footnote in this story. In the seventeenth century, when the colonies were swiftly settled by people looking for (their own) religious liberty, colonists took for granted the integration of religious and public life. In Puritan New England, separating the sacred from the secular was as impossible as finding the line between night and day. In the 1600s, churches owned no property; they met in the town "meetinghouse" – an architectural innovation – owned by taxpayers, designed for all public gatherings, from raucous town meetings to somber church services. One 1654 document called a "house for the town" – the seat of the town's economic, political, and social life – the most appropriate place for worship.[19] Meanwhile, the lands surrounding the meetinghouse (including burial

---

[19] The churches worshiping in meetinghouses were those favored by the state; dissenters met in people's homes. Kevin M. Sweeney, "Meetinghouses, Townhouses, and Churches: Changing Perceptions of Sacred and Secular Space in Southern New England, 1720-1850," *Winterthur Portfolio* 28 (Spring 1993), 60.

grounds) doubled as public parks for human leisure and public pastures for grazing livestock.

In the 1720s, a shift began that transformed New England meetinghouses into what we now recognize as "churches" – sacred buildings dedicated entirely to God. Meetinghouses began to banish civic meetings from their spaces. Town meetings, deemed too rowdy for sacred spaces, moved to taverns and, eventually, to their own dedicated town halls.[20] Steeples were added to most meetinghouses; the meetinghouse's domed ceiling, originally meant to improve acoustics, became a symbol of heaven, stretching across a room now reserved exclusively for worship. The meetinghouse door was moved from the middle of the long side of the building to the east end, with the pulpit opposite, facing the rising sun (i.e., the risen Son/Christ). In the 1790s, the people of Pittsfield, Massachusetts – like scores of their neighbors – voted to stop using the cemetery as a pasture, and banned any game "played with a ball" within eighty yards of the meetinghouse, because the "temple of God should never be exposed to profanation."[21]

This effort to honor God with designated space, undefiled by the messy "publick," was spectacularly successful in one sense: by 1800, most colonial churches had their own "sacred" buildings, set apart from public life. But in one important way, the movement backfired badly: churches became synonymous with their buildings, and the concern for the broader parish,

---

[20] By the end of the 18th century, romanticism, with its emphasis on sensuality and nature, and the First Great Awakening, with its "piety of sensation," had swept the young nation, supplanting austere Puritan aesthetics and sensibilities. By the mid-1800s, weddings and funerals had become religious ceremonies. (Before the eighteenth century, these were strictly civic events; weddings were performed in homes by magistrates, not ministers; the "funeral sermon" was preached at the next regular Sunday service following a death). See Sweeney, 66.

[21] Sweeney, 83-84.

or neighborhood, faded. The holier we got, the less useful we became. Historian Kevin Sweeney notes: "As the sanctity of exclusively religious space grew, [the church] grew more marginal in the shared public life of communities where commerce, politics, and other cultural activities increased in importance."[22] Soon the town hall – not the church – became the town's symbolic source of unity. The town hall became something else as well – a *de facto* temple for an emerging and competing new faith: American civil religion.[23]

To be sure, Americans were not alone in limiting Christianity's substantial creative energies to what happened behind church doors. After a century of institution-building religious energy and global social reform on the part of Catholic sisters, the Vatican decreed in 1900 that active religious women must embrace the cloister. By 1917, sisters' lives were defined by canon law, which imposed set times for prayers and Eucharist, travel restrictions, and prohibitions on going out alone (kind of an ecclesial equivalent to keeping women "barefoot and pregnant" so they would not "stray"). Nuns worked in the schools and hospitals that they founded but control was given over to priests. As one sister put it, "Everyday life got smaller. Religious life became a celebration of the trivial."[24] After a century when religious women created, advocated for, and led hospitals, colleges, foundations, schools, and charities, pioneered new knowledge and created new systems of care, these restrictions "reaffirmed the view from Rome that religious life takes place in the convent,

---

22 Sweene, 93.

23 Sweeney, 86.

24 Sioban Nelson, *Say Little, Do Much: Nursing, Nuns and Hospitals in the Nineteenth Century* (Philadelphia: University of Pennsylvania Press, 2001), 157.

as opposed to the streets, hospitals wards, and homes of the poor." According to historian Sioban Nelson, as prohibitions on movement increased, "the pioneering achievements of the nineteenth century became less and less possible to repeat."[25] Not until 1962 were religious women allowed to face the world again, thanks to the reforms of Vatican II.

So, we cannot blame the government alone for removing religion from public life in the United States; churches helped. The disestablishment clause was variously interpreted (for Thomas Jefferson it was a "wall" of separation between church and state; for James Madison, it was a "line"), but the "wall" idea prevailed. Even as the clause has famously protected religious practice in the United States, churches have widely misread it as a warning not to venture beyond their property lines. As Thomas Groome observes, an unfortunate consequence has been the insinuation that we must somehow "transcend the influence" of our spirituality in public life.[26] The result was the near suffocation of ministry for the common good in American churches. With each passing century, ministry became confined to narrower and narrower lanes. By the 21st century, charity was deemed an appropriate way to exercise faith in public, but enterprise was suspect; ceremonial religious participation was tolerated in public, but personal religious expressions like wearing hijabs in the workplace, were often frowned upon.

---

[25] Nelson, 157.

[26] Thomas Groome, *Sharing Faith: A Comprehensive Approach to Religious Education and Pastoral Ministry* (Eugene, OR: Wipf and Stock, 1999), 15. Groome is specifically addressing the influence of faith on education.

Desperation as Spiritual Gift: The Great Loosening

As Benoit Godin points out, what churches feared throughout history was not innovation; they feared innovation's *effects*.[27] People don't fear novelty; they fear *change*. Today, many American Christians are unsure how to bear witness to Christ authentically but indirectly. Proselytization – a screamingly direct, and almost always inappropriate, form of religious communication – is all we know, usually from disastrous examples. As a result, we often consider churches "innovative" when they practice indirect forms of witness well because they *do* faithfully interact with their communities in significant ways, cultivating sustainable economic engines, creating novel collaborations with multiple and even non-religious partners. These ministries feel fresh and original simply because indirect witness has become unusual for most congregations, whose primary models of witness in the public square require proselytizing, charity, or both.

The good news is that, after 300 years of tightening our ecclesial corsets, the church is experiencing a noticeable "loosening" in terms of what ministry entails. Desperation is a spiritual gift; dwindling memberships, closed bank accounts, and diminishing moral sway have caused some churches to reassess their mission, unlearning and relearning how to follow Jesus in their current contexts. Sometimes we are so eager for change that we venture into conversations about entrepreneurship and new partnerships naively; churches want to jump onto the latest trend, or we want to "save the world" (or the church), or we think social innovation will solve our congregation's financial or marketing problems (spoiler alert: none of these work).

But if we stop opposing the sacred and the secular, we can set in motion a virtuous cycle, illustrated by a church meeting I had today. St. Bartholomew Lutheran Church sits in a struggling neighborhood in Trenton, New Jersey that is 95% Hispanic. The church, too, is struggling; they have a part-time pastor and about 35 on a Sunday – until recently, all Anglos. The church's precarious finances weigh heavily on St. Bart's young pastor, the Rev. Erich Kussman. But when the pandemic revealed raging food insecurity in Trenton, Erich was certain that Jesus was calling St. Bart's to feed people. The church food pantry, which normally saw about 20 people a week, was suddenly serving hundreds. So, Erich reached out to surrounding churches, including ours, to donate food.

As Erich got to know people using the pantry, he realized something else: many of them were there because of school closures. Neighborhood children were no longer getting hot meals at school. Lunch became another meal strapped parents had to pull together. Erich wondered if Jesus was calling St. Bart's to get lunch to these kids. So, he called on his network of churches, and asked us to pack lunches.

St. Bart's began distributing hundreds of bag lunches, and Erich noticed some people taking seven or eight bags. He investigated. Turns out, the reason was the internet. Internet is wildly erratic in lower-income communities in Trenton – so when schools closed for the pandemic, kids gathered for online classes in whatever house had an internet signal, where they ate lunch together. Erich wondered if Jesus wanted St. Bart's to help these kids access their online classes with better

The Black Church Food Security Network

Baltimore, Maryland

When the 2015 protests erupted in Baltimore over Freddie Gray's death at the hands of police, schools and shops were burned and looted, and roads were shut down to contain the violence. For many people in the city, it was impossible to travel – which made it impossible to get food. Hungry people went to Pleasant Hope Baptist Church for help.

A few years earlier, Pleasant Hope had converted its manicured lawn into a community garden to address diet-related illnesses in the neighborhood. Now they were being asked to address another food crisis. When calls from cut-off neighborhoods came in, Pleasant Hope's young pastor, the Rev. Dr. Heber Brown III, put out a plea to black farmers in surrounding rural areas of Maryland: Bring your wares to the church, and we'll box them up for people cut off from their food supply.

It worked. *The Black Church Food Security Network* was born.

It has been said, "Whoever controls the food controls the people." Brown realized that food sovereignty was a key form of empowerment for disenfranchised communities, and that black churches could use their land to end what he calls *food apartheid* – a system that affects more than just those unable to buy quality food. Black farmers often struggle to find buyers and bear the brunt of environmental racism, involuntary land loss, and discrimination in planning/public policy. By linking black farmers to black consumers, the BCFSN helps both.

The BCFSN supports churches starting gardens on their land, establishes pop-up produce stands before/after church and connects black farmers to black churches to stock their stands. Brown emphasizes: this is not charity (even Pleasant Hope's produce is sold at the church market). The enterprise model challenges the have/have-not divide perpetuated by charity. At Pleasant Hope's market, one urban farmer sold out of her produce in under two hours; at the city's farmers market, she sold for six hours without breaking even.

Reports often describe the BCFSN as an "innovative" solution – but it aims for bigger: to build a sustainable, community-centered food system anchored by black churches and black food producers, and led by those most directly affected by economic inequity. Brown recognizes that food is just the beginning, "It's an ecosystem for spiritual joy and social justice," he said. "If we can grow food together and feed ourselves, what else can we do together?"

internet service. So now he is figuring out how to boost the church's internet signal and make the church building a neighborhood internet hub.

There's more. While distributing lunches, Erich found out that no one in the neighborhood – hotel workers, restaurant staff, custodians – had received a single government stimulus check throughout the pandemic. Erich thought maybe Jesus wanted St. Bart's to help their neighbors pay their bills. So, he and some other community workers spent two weeks at the Statehouse, advocating for the distribution of stimulus checks to their zip code.

As Erich pleaded the case of his parish to lawmakers, people in the neighborhood who had never attended worship at St. Bart's began to feel like St. Bart's was their church. When St. Bart's started outdoor worship services in the spring of 2020, the services doubled in size. Half of the congregation spoke Spanish. Erich was pretty sure Jesus wanted St. Bart's to help people worship. So, he asked a volunteer if she would translate, and now St. Bart's services are bilingual.

Is St. Bart's innovating? Maybe not yet – nothing Erich has done so far is new. *But it is new for St. Bart's.* St. Bart's new prophetic imagination for the neighborhood was made possible simply because the pastor got to know the church's neighbors. Compared to the insular congregation it was 12 months ago, St. Bart's is pioneering some massive changes. Erich did not set out to innovate; he set out to feed people. He is a long way from having a sustainable plan. But indirect witness has set in motion a virtuous cycle that is helping St. Bart's become a dramatically more imaginative church. As the church became involved in the neighborhood, previously unimaginable friendships were formed, and previously overlooked needs were noticed. New friends became co-conspirators in helping neighbors thrive. This transformed the church from being a neighborhood service provider to becoming a neighborhood stakeholder, invested in the community's well-being. Stakeholders read Scripture with different eyes than service providers; worship and spiritual practices are viewed from a new slant, which provides fresh energy for discipleship. Newly invigorated disciples follow Jesus into the neighborhood even further, where they make more friends, and notice more felt needs – and the cycle continues.

Erich Kussman took a bank shot. He aimed for love, not innovation – and love made St. Bart's try something new. To be clear, Erich is totally making this up as he goes. But as he follows Jesus further into the neighborhood, he is not only helping St. Bart's feed people. He is helping them resist the inertia of insularity, and the numbness that comes from being cut off from the public square, which have sapped dry the energy and imagination of countless congregations.

The real crisis facing North American Christianity is not a lack of resources, but a lack of imagination – the "lift" that frees us from being entangled by the fatalistic stories that our economic, cultural, and political systems foist upon us. With each step into the community, St. Bart's imagination grows larger as the congregation confronts deeper problems, each of which requires more in the way of ingenuity. Slowly, this little church is beginning to innovate – to imagine and implement an alternative reality in the spirit of Jesus: a vision of Trenton as a city where no one is hungry, children can

The Parish Collective

Seattle, WA

In Spokane, Washington, there's a bench on Oak Street that is smothered in color. In June 2019, some neighbors (part of the Spokane Collective of *The Parish Collective* movement) had a block party. Hauling an old church pew onto the street with paints and brushes, they invited people to cover the pew in images and words that responded to the question: "What is the neighborhood you hope for?"

Today the bench welcomes neighbors to take a break, and Lauren Goldbloom notices lots of people stopping to take it in. She confesses, "I get emotional when I look at it." There are rainbows and hearts, words like justice, peace, and compassion, images of one hand lifting another, and a garden blooming through a rainstorm. She reflects on the trauma of 2020 and the need for honesty and healing. But the bench reminds her of how people's hopes for a neighborhood can bring them together.

The conviction that God works through neighborhoods is at the core of *The Parish Collective*, a network connecting churches, faith-based organizations, and other entities around neighborhood reconciliation and parish renewal. "We're on a campaign to say that we think God is organizing the church around the neighborhood," says co-founder Tim Soerens. "Where is the church on a Tuesday afternoon? Can you see it...in any meaningful sense?"

Parish initiatives don't aim for social innovation, but for connections – but in so doing they have ignited countless creative, sustainable ministries in the service of "community weaving." Initiatives might come from traditional congregations like *New Canaan Community Church* in the West Englewood neighborhood of Chicago, or "new monastic" communities like *SoulSpace* in Australia – described as "a bunch of people who live and do life together" – to out-of-the-box ministries like *Storywagon*, Chaplain Jose Martinez's mobile studio/podcast ministry (housed in a VW van).

Because *The Parish Collective* connects imaginative people as well as neighborhoods, they resource each other's creativity. But Soerens insists that God's imagination is already present in neighborhoods. "The place to start," says Soerens, "is not with a church question but with a God question, 'How might God be working in my neighborhood?' If you could just showcase or put a light on all of the followers of Jesus who already love God and love their neighbors and neighborhoods, we'd be overwhelmed."

learn, people can pay their bills and come together to praise God, no matter what language they speak.

The take-away from all of this is that innovation follows mission, not the other way around. The entire history of the church can be read this way: Jesus was an innovation for Judaism, Paul innovated for the Gentiles, the early church innovated new attitudes toward the inclusion of the poor and the marginalized, and medieval monastic communities experimented with everything from champagne to education and democratic process.[28] None of these developments happened because Christians tried to "be innovative." They happened because Christians tried to be *the church* – to tell all the Truth, and tell it slant by addressing their communities' deepest hungers in the way of Jesus. In so doing, they discovered what every mother already knows: love innovates.

Prophetic Innovation: How to Orbit the Giant Hairball

If we were to map St. Bart's efforts on the innovation continuum (see Figure 3.1), it would be on the low-risk left – imitation, improvement, moving toward evolution. St. Bart's has a long way to go before it becomes disruptive or revolutionary, though at this rate, those may be coming. Without the neighborhood pulling St. Bart's away from its gravitational center (the existing congregation), change will inevitably spring back to the left of the continuum. Every system must maintain itself, so instigating change requires us to overshoot our mark slightly, knowing that the inertia of systems

---

[28] Cf., "Monasteries in the High Middle Ages as Powerhouses of Innovation: Designs for Living and Models of Social and Legal Order in Europe," *Heidelberger Akademie der Wissenschaften* (research summary), http://www.haw.uni-heidelberg.de/forschung/forschungsstellen/kloester. en.html (accessed July 11, 2016).

will always tug us back toward the status quo. If we don't overshoot, the gravitational pull of the hairball will suck us backward, and nothing will change. If we overshoot too far, we will spin out into deep space, where no one can hear us advocate for something new.

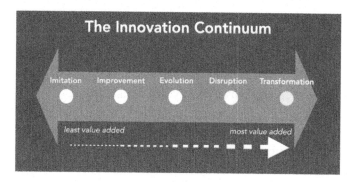

Figure 3.1

The "Hairball" is what Gordon Mackenzie, former Hallmark "Creative Paradox" (his actual title), called the organizations and systems in which we work. In his unconventional classic on corporate survival, *Orbiting the Giant Hairball,* Mackenzie illustrates the Hairball (there are pictures) as a tangled, impenetrable mass of rules, traditions, and systems, all based on what worked in the past.[29] This past has enormous gravity: "We've always done it that way." The Hairball's gravitational pull nullifies new insights and potential creative breakthroughs by sucking us into its center. In the Hairball, every bird is a chicken: we can flap our wings, but we can't fly.

The opposite of the Hairball is deep space. If we

29   Gordon Mackenzie, *Orbiting the Giant Hairball* (New York: Viking Books), 1998.

distance ourselves too far from the Hairball, we float off, our insights and potential contributions lost to oblivion, where they are no help to anyone. The reality is that humans love Hairballs; we help create them. In some ways they deserve our compassion. So, the trick is not to obliterate a stultifying Hairball, or even to change it (for Mackenzie, this is futile; our efforts just ensnare us further), but to find a place of balance where we benefit from the physical, intellectual, and philosophical resources of an organization "without becoming entombed in the bureaucracy of an institution."[30]

Mackenzie's advice is to *orbit* the Hairball, which for him is a practice of "responsible creativity," vigorously exploring and operating beyond the Hairball's accepted models, patterns, or standards – all the while staying connected to the spirit of its mission. As Mackenzie says: "To be of optimum value to the corporate endeavor, you must invest enough individuality to counteract the pull of Corporate Gravity, but not so much that you escape this pull altogether. Just enough to stay out of the hairball." In fact, we need a dynamic relationship with the Hairball, which makes its gravity an asset: it keeps us from "flying off into the overwhelming nothingness of deep space."[31] It is in this creative tension between the Hairball and deep space – between individuality and corporate conformity, between leveraging the Hairball's resources and being smothered by them, between being absorbed by the Hairball and harnessing its gifts – that innovation takes place.

Mackenzie misses an even more radical option, because even he cannot imagine it: the *transformation*

---

[30]   Mackenzie, 33.

[31]   Mackenzie, 33.

of the Hairball's center of gravity. He is right that our efforts to untangle the Hairball are doomed; yet this is precisely what God is up to in Jesus Christ. Jesus shot straight to the middle of the messiest hairball of them all, human existence, and allowed himself, literally, to become entombed by it – until he didn't. In the resurrection, Jesus defied the Hairball's gravitational force, bursting through its treacly straps with us in tow, energizing a new future.[32] What's more, following Jesus sometimes means following him right into the Hairball's command center, to be prophets of possibility who proclaim a different kind of existence. Lashed to Christ, the Hairball cannot claim us. Jesus does not remove the Hairball, but he provides a way out – a way to escape its gravitational pull that does not require us to achieve lift-off on our own. Jesus makes a way for chickens to fly.

Innovation and the Prophetic Imagination

Walter Brueggemann views innovation as implementing a prophetic imagination. He is not shy about his admiration of Moses as an innovator.[33] For Brueggemann, prophetic ministry evokes, forms, reforms and implements an alternative consciousness to that of the dominant culture – which might also be described as the aim of Christian social innovation.[34] To Brueggemann, innovation is the gift of productive tension between past and possibility: "The prophet

---

[32] See Walter Brueggemann, *The Prophetic Imagination*, 40th Anniversary Ed. (Minneapolis: Fortress, 2018), 3.

[33] "The newness and radical innovations of Moses and Israel in this period can hardly be over-stated...*The appearance of a new social reality* is unprecedented." Brueggemann, 5-6.

[34] Brueggemann, 3.

lives in tension with the tradition. While the prophet is indeed shaped by the tradition, breaking free from the tradition to assert the new freedom of God is also characteristic of the prophet."[35] Brueggemann maintains that the most critical problems prophets must address are not specific crises like war or hunger, but the crisis of imagination that leaves religious people, including American churches, demoralized, dehumanized, and numb.

Brueggemann points out that "imagination must come before implementation,"[36] but we cannot imagine possibilities we have not seen. The power of Christian social innovation lies in illustration: by embodying the life, death, and resurrection of Jesus in various ways, we show a different possibility for being human that, through Jesus, now lies within reach. Jesus painted his innovative vision – the Reign of God – in every sermon, parable, and relationship of his short time on earth. And when he did, tombs opened, dry bones danced, and dead people lived. Newness was born.

So what might that look like for us?

---

[35] "The prophet is called to be a child of the tradition, one who has taken it seriously in the shaping of his or her own field of perception and system of language, who is so at home in that memory that the points of contact and incongruity with the situation of the church in culture can be discerned and articulated with proper urgency." Walter Brueggemann, *The Prophetic Imagination*, 2nd edition (Minneapolis: Fortress, 2001), 2. For more on traditioned innovation, see L. Gregory Jones and Andrew P. Hogue, *Navigating the Future: Traditioned Innovation for Wilder Seas* (Nashville: Abingdon), 2021.

[36] Brueggemann, 40.

Conversations

- How has Love made you an inventor? Who is Love calling you to invent for now?

- How well does your church practice indirect witness in the public square? How (and to whom) might God be calling you to "tell all the Truth, but tell it slant" right now?

- Remember Episcopal Bishop Michael Curry's remark: "If it doesn't look like Jesus of Nazareth, then it can't be called Christian." How does the ministry you are imagining for people in your neighborhood look like Jesus?

What Next?

If your group or Expedition Team is starting to consider the problems in your community that break your heart, or if you're beginning to have a few ideas for addressing these problems, now is a good time to begin a discernment process. You can use either or both of these exercises:

- Do *The Wagon Wheel* on p. 157 (This exercise works best with 10 or more people, though it can be adapted for smaller groups. Individuals will benefit from the questions.)

- Play the game *Ripple Effect* by Discipleship by Design. Use it with a team of 3-8, or have a congregational "Game and Discernment" night, with a few boards going at once.

If your group is doing this exercise as part of The Great Expedition: Circle back around to Kibbey's *Open Road* to consider a breakthrough prayer initiative for what you are discovering in your community. Use Nixon's Cultural Competence resource to be reminded of how to build relationships within your community.

To download *The Wagon Wheel*, order *Ripple Effect*, or get more information, go to www.ministryincubators.com.

CHAPTER FOUR

No Going Back to the Shire: Innovating on Innovation

"You know what your problem is? I will tell you what it is. You just don't have any idea how low God's standards are. They are very low...very, very low, indeed. Remember, you cannot do anything to make God love you more, and you cannot do anything to make God love you less.

Archbishop Desmond Tutu[1]

"Excellence is the creepiest word in ministry."

A graduating seminarian

Every now and then, it is good to be reminded that God doesn't call any of us into ministry, professional or otherwise, because we're good at it. A quick glance through the Scriptural address book of God's chosen is humbling: not a valedictorian among them, not a single CEO on the list. God reliably seeks the unlikeliest candidate available, and zooms in. Abraham and Jacob, scumbags both, were chosen to sire a nation and to establish Israel, respectively. Moses – murderer on the lam – was so unprepared to meet Pharaoh that God gave him a multi-talented team. David, the youngest of a strapping band of brothers, was so unlikely to be chosen

---

[1] Attributed. Brian Mahan, *Forgetting Ourselves on Purpose* (San Francisco: Jossey-Bass), 2002.

king that he wasn't even invited to the anointing party. Weepy Jeremiah was chosen for prophetic leadership before he was born, and therefore before there was any evidence *whatsoever* that he was cut out for this kind of thing. And Mary, an unwed pregnant preteen from a poor family (and a woman, let's not forget), got the biggest assignment of them all: mother of God, *theotokos* – not exactly a story people were likely to believe.

We are in excellent company.

As we fumble around, figuring out boat building plans, this conversation about Christian social innovation should not sit too easily. We are always in danger of inviting Trojan horses into the sanctuary, elevating excellence over discipleship, production over prayer, heroism over humility. It is not always clear whether we are being a prophet or a pied piper; both promise people better futures, and both usually sound a little crazy. How do we know whether this wilderness leads anywhere, much less to freedom – or if it's time to pack up the timbrels and return to Egypt, where our worth is easily measured by the quality of our bricks? The learning curve for anything new is steep, even when it grows out of a long heritage. What if we dance with the wrong partner, succumb to the sirens, or fail to recognize the big bad wolf? Worse, what if we inadvertently *contribute* to the soul-crushing patterns of life that we earnestly want to disrupt, by creating yet another way to be more efficient and effective?[2] What if all this work in innovation moves us further from God, and makes churches more dysfunctional, not less?

Short of being sealed in a hermitage (a weird but faithful choice for some), I know of no way to avoid these

---

[2]   See Andrew Root, *The Congregation in the Secular Age* (Grand Rapids: Baker Academic), 2021.

risks in any ministry. More than one ministry has been funded by a Ponzi scheme, and countless cults have smuggled the seeds of treachery inside good intentions.[3] It is always seductive to want to "maximize our potential" (think of all the good we could do) instead of nurturing a vision of "the good life" that Jesus refused to equate with productivity. And, by way of reminder, being a dysfunctional faith community has not, so far, stopped God from working through them. Faith is as likely to take root amid turmoil as tranquility, and God is a famous upcycler. Humans, after all, came from mud.

Every paradigm shift that has confronted the church – the persecution and then legalization of Christianity, the mystics' move to the desert, monasticism's development as communities, the Protestant Reformation's endorsement of married clergy, the disestablishment of religion in the United States, to name a few – has had economic, social, and political consequences that altered church practices and changed the way Christians approach the surrounding culture. The answers change, but the church's question is always the same, shipwreck or no shipwreck: "How might we become Christ's body – the embodiment of God's love for the world – for people in these particular conditions, at this particular moment in time?"

[3] Cf. Sharon Walsh, "After 2 Years, the Whistle's Heard," *The Washington Post* (May 18, 1995), https://www.washingtonpost.com/archive/business/1995/05/18/after-2-years-the-whistles-heard/d1e78bac-0c83-4ae4-9265-7b4fa3c93547/. Jim Jones, the notorious cult leader who led The Peoples Temple in a murder/suicide ritual in Guyana in 1978, was a civil rights leader; many joined The Peoples Temple because of its commitment to interracial harmony. Cf. Rebecca Moore, "Before the Tragedy at Jonestown, the Peoples Temple Had a Dream," *The Conversation* (November 16, 2018), https://theconversation.com/before-the-tragedy-at-jonestown-the-people-of-peoples-temple-had-a-dream-103151 (both accessed April 27, 2021).

No Going Back to the Shire

I believe the American church – and I am speaking
of Christian bodies in the United States, though I
suspect we are not alone – is experiencing the birth
pangs of another paradigm shift, in which monumental
changes both within the church and within the broader
culture are decisively altering the ways we relate
to one another. COVID-19 was not the origin of this
shift – we have smelled it coming for decades – but it
will be the moment we point to when the cracks in the
current system became visible even to people outside
of churches. It may also be the moment we point to say,
*"That was the time. That was when things changed: a
crack opened, and love rushed in. That was the moment
when God started using churches in a new way."*

The church is at its best in times of crisis, and 2020
was no exception. Between quarantines, profound
grief, economic hardship, and cultural tensions, many
churches stepped out from behind their programs and
services (*double entendre* intended). There was nothing
else to do except to *be with* people, to be a nimble "ark of
salvation" for traumatized souls looking for sanctuary
as we muddled through the storm. Liturgy gave us some
toeholds, a way to mark the seasons when all we could
see was fog. Everything else was thrown overboard.
In some ways, this period of loss made us more like
the church Jesus calls us to be than we have been in
centuries. The ark took a beating, to be sure. We're still
figuring out what to repair and what to replace. Until
then, here we are: washed up in an unfamiliar cultural
moment. Our boat is full of holes and our compass is
broken, and strangers are headed our way.

I am inviting us to see all of this as a divine gift.
Change has found *us*.

We are weary, of course, but not because of the pandemic. With some exceptions, congregations in the United States have been unsustainable for some time. Here on Malta, we are free to abandon our least faithful choices and discern alternatives, and gather up (as theologian Willie Jennings provocatively puts it) "unused gospel lying all around."[4] As I see it, the COVID-shaken church has two choices: to patch things up and row back to where we came from, or to become the church Christ calls us to be, imagining and embodying a new kind of life-giving community for our current situation. It's not much of a choice. The fragility of American institutional life has been laid bare, and there is no unseeing the man behind the curtain. To paraphrase Frodo Baggins, there is no going back to the shire – for even if we *were* to find it unchanged, *we* are not the same.[5]

The Prophetic Tasks of Innovation

This is the part where you get impatient: "So what do we *do?*" In this chapter, I suggest that Christians' unique take on innovation, our participation in God's "new thing," presents us with a peculiar opportunity. We can use this moment to "innovate on innovation": to rescue innovation's meaning from its commercial captivity and recast Christian social innovation as love – specifically as participation in God's endlessly creative, self-giving love that energizes new life.[6] Lashing ourselves to the cross with Jesus allows us to participate in human cultural systems as prophets, not captives. Thanks to the promise of resurrection, we can

---

[4] Willie Jennings, *After Whiteness: An Education in Belonging* (Grand Rapids: Eerdmans, 2020), 133.

[5] J.R.R. Tolkien, *The Return of the King* (New York: Del Ray, 2012), 379.

[6] Walter Brueggemann, *The Prophetic Imagination,* 2nd edition (Minneapolis: Fortress, 2001), 4-5.

Mortar

Cincinnati, Ohio

In 2001, a white police officer shot an unarmed black teenager in Cincinnati's Over-the-Rhine neighborhood, igniting days of riots. By 2009, OTR – as locals call it – was dubbed "the most dangerous neighborhood in America." Today the neighborhood, once the hub of Cincinnati's brewery district, is one of the most popular districts in the city. It is a haven for historic preservations, new businesses (including breweries), and arts and culture. It is also a magnet for young professionals – and an area of intense gentrification.

Derrick Braziel and William Thomas met in college. Thomas is an OTR native; he didn't want to see OTR natives pushed out as wealthier people moved in. Thomas knew that people in OTR had great ideas but often lacked the know-how to launch and grow them. He and Braziel saw entrepreneurship as a way to change lives. At *Mortar*, Braziel says, "loving God's people comes through the idea of giving them space for their ideas to be developed."

In 2014, *Mortar* was founded as an incubator to help historically marginalized entrepreneurs build enterprises just steps from their homes. Partnering with churches and other local organizations, *Mortar* offers affordable courses in entrepreneurship, access to grants and loans, retail space for pop-up shops, and a community of mentors and other early-stage entrepreneurs who work together to overcome the obstacles to starting a business.

Braziel and Thomas view *Mortar* as a calling. Braziel remembers reading Ecclesiastes 9:4 ("Anyone who is among the living has hope") and being convicted that hope required economic, social, and racial justice: "I knew I needed to dedicate my life to supporting black and brown people using the love and promise of God."

In 2020, Braziel and Thomas stepped down from *Mortar* (which is now being replicated in five other cities) to follow their entrepreneurial dreams. Since its founding, *Mortar* has graduated nearly 300 neighborhood businesses (e.g., *Esoteric Brewing*, *Black Owned*, *Sweets & Meats Barbecue*) and nonprofits like the *Real Deal Boxing Club*, an after-school program that teaches kids boxing while building confidence, providing community, and helping them realize "that someone will always be in their corner." As OTR is revitalized with bricks and mortar, Braziel and Thomas have made sure that the real mortar of communities – people – are amply supplied with hope, networks, and opportunities.

follow Jesus into the messiest parts of human existence to describe what reality looks like from *beyond* the hairball, confident that the hairball – even if it kills us – cannot claim us.

Brueggemann argues that prophetic work is creative work, taking place in the tension between critiquing the world as we know it, and re-energizing it. To do that, every prophet has three tasks: naming *reality*, *grief*, and *hope*.[7] This framework guides Christian social innovators, too, as we look for ways to implement a prophetic imagination.

Naming reality, and exposing the myths we use to disguise that reality, is the first step. This is a thankless task, because like King Ahab (2 Chron. 18:1-7), we hate prophets that bring bad news. What's more, naming reality is harder than it sounds, since every worldview is built upon scores of unspoken assumptions that we fail to notice or conveniently overlook. For example, Christian leaders gobble up business resources, presumably to help us name realities about ministry, without realizing that many of those resources are predicated on economic assumptions (e.g., growth at all costs, the idol of productivity, profit before people, and so on) that are utterly at odds with Jesus' vision. But just as no entrepreneur wants to hear that late consumer culture is vile (it is, but that's another conversation), neither do most pastors want the job of extricating their congregations from our late capitalist hairball (that is both impossible and way too easy). Far simpler to stay on the surface, and name only what we see.

When we are in denial about our present reality,

---

[7] Walter Brueggemann, *Reality, Grief, Hope: Three Urgent Prophetic Tasks* (Grand Rapids, MI: Eerdmans), 2014.

an alternative vision – even one offered by Jesus – feels unnecessary. That is why prophetic work requires a second task: grief. Prophets name present realities that the dominant culture is sure to deny, making it is almost impossible for us to let go of our accustomed worldview in favor of a "new thing" offered by God or anybody else (especially when the present reality benefits us). So, we must grieve losing our romanticized version of reality in order to grasp the reality we actually have. Brueggemann reminds us that the Hebrew prophets confronted this problem as a matter of course. Since cultural awakening was part of their job description, prophets had to be a wildly creative lot. They tried stunt after stunt to pierce people's denial. Weird theatrics, fits of fury to demonstrate God's wrath, awkward public appearances, righteous solidarity with the vulnerable – all of these were goads in the prophetic toolbox. But at the end of the day, says Brueggemann, what finally makes people stop and question their denial is not persuasion, but grief.

Grief defies analysis or theologizing; managing grief feels obscene to the one in mourning. But grief loosens our bolts. Things that once felt important no longer seem that way. Convictions we once built our lives around now raise questions. Grief is the antidote to denial.[8] For an illustration, look to the George Floyd case of 2020-2021. Racism has been the worm in the apple of America's self-perception since slavery – yet it has been nearly impossible to shatter the systems that protect racism in the United States. This is our present reality, and endless attempts to name that reality in recent years have barely moved the needle on attitudes

---

[8] Brueggemann, *Reality, Grief, Hope*, 57.

toward race in the United States.

It was the release of a cell phone video, shot by a traumatized teenager witnessing a black man's suffocation by a white police officer, that unleashed a tsunami of grief, and punctured many Americans' denial. The video named the reality, but it was grief – losing a false image of ourselves that "we are better than this" – that made us believe it. No one expected the grief over George Floyd's murder to end American racism, or even to make a sizable dent. It was a pinprick – but it was enough to take some air out of our culture's vaunted denials of racism, which opened many people to imagining a different future.

Grief slows us down. As Brueggemann teaches us, it is the prophet's job to encourage, engage, and participate in a public grief over loss. Unacknowledged grief turns to rage which leads to violence; recognized grief leads to lament, which is why Brueggemann urges us to pay attention to lament whenever we hear it: in Scripture and in the streets, among the marginalized and among people fresh from despair. Grief reminds us why Christian social innovation responds to the *who* before the *why*. It challenges our impulse to hurry up and "fix" things by reconnecting us to the limits of being human, and by making room for loss and disappointment. We would much rather just pull the covers back up – but Christian social innovation cannot afford that, and a prophetic imagination will not allow it. Grief helps us get straight, at least for a moment, who is God and who is not.

The third prophetic task is the reason for the others: naming *hope*. Even the gloomiest prophet offers the community "an alternative consciousness" that energizes it for new forms of faithfulness and vitality. This is the innovative vision we have been describing.

The Dinner Party

Grieving While Breaking Bread

My peers have trouble relating to what I've been through, so it's cathartic to be with others who get this aspect of what I'm living with…We all show up with pent-up emotions and…share the strong and complicated feelings we have. It feels healing and transformative to be together.

That's how 29-year-old Sam, who lost his dad to suicide, described *The Dinner Party*, a worldwide community of 20 and 30 somethings who break bread together and share stories of loss. You need two qualifications to join a dinner party: be a young adult and have an experience of traumatic loss – usually the death of a parent, partner, child, sibling, or close friend.

Before COVID-19, dinners were in-person potluck meals. Hundreds of hosts welcomed young adults – strangers – into their homes, who had found the meeting time/place on an app and showed up with a dish to share. No one tries to "fix" or advise. Over time strangers become friends, connected by more than experiences of loss. (Churches replicating this model may use an in-person option, but *The Dinner Party* app now connects people online, through "buddy systems" and "virtual tables.")

The Dinner Party is a secular 501(c)(3), not a ministry; it has no faith affiliation. But its non-medicalized approach to healing has inspired dinner churches and congregations hoping to create safe communities for struggling people. (A sister organization, *The People's Supper*, was founded by pastors and theology students who worked with *The Dinner Party* founder Lennon Flowers Patinkin to bring people of opposing political views together – over dinner, of course – after the 2016 election. So far more than 10,000 people have gathered around tables in 100 cities).

The Eucharist makes creating and protecting sacred space around the table intuitive for most congregations (it is also a fitting context for processing death and loss). Young adults skeptical of organized religion enjoy communion over meals, with each other, if not with God. As FlowersPatinkin says: "We are still looking for spaces where we can talk about what we normally would have shared with a priest." (*The Dinner Party* has compiled a resource manual with other rituals, from multiple faith traditions, that help people grieve; see insert bibliography). As one participant put it: "It's about feeling like other people are helping me carry my burden and in exchange, I take on some of theirs, which is always lighter than my own."

The prophetic task, Brueggemann reminds us, is to "declare and enact hope for a buoyant future that is securely in the purview of God."[9]

Christians understand this alternative consciousness as *agape*, the last-shall-be-first, weak-shall-be-strong, meek-shall-inherit-the-earth vision of Jesus.[10] Jesus did everything backwards, eating with sinners and plucking grain on the Sabbath. When John the Baptist's followers wanted to know if Jesus was the One they had been waiting for (asking for a friend), Jesus sends back the Messianic signature:

> *Go and tell John what you have seen and heard: the blind receive their sight, the lame walk, the lepers are cleansed, the deaf hear, the dead are raised, the poor have good news brought to them.*

Luke 7:22

---

[9]   Brueggemann, *Reality, Grief, Hope,* 101.

[10] For Kraybill, the upside-down vision of agape calls into question "business as usual" in provocative ways:
    "We are the folks who engage in conspicuous sharing...
    Our faith wags our pocketbooks.
    We give without expecting a return.
    We forgive liberally as God forgave us.
    We overlook the signs of stigma hanging on the unlovely.
    Genuine compassion for the poor and destitute moves us.
    We look and move down the ladder.
    We don't take our religious structures too seriously because we know Jesus is Lord...
    We serve rather than dominate.
    We invite rather than coerce.
    Love replaces hate among us.
    Shalom overcomes revenge...
    We share power, love assertively, make peace.
    We flatten hierarchies and behave like children...
    Servant structures replace rigid hierarchies...
    We join in a common life for worship and support.
    Here we discern the times and the issues
    In the common life we discover
    the Spirit's direction for our individual and corporate ministries."
    Donald Kraybill, *The Upside-Down Kingdom* (Harrisonburg, VA: Herald Press, 2012), 255.

It's an artistic response, on Jesus' part – he tells all the Truth, but tells it slant. Hope is more evocative than provocative, more art than science, more poetry than progress report.[11] But we can be sure that the Messiah is in our midst when we confront a vision that turns human reality-as-we-know-it on its head: stories of hope overtake tales of despair, and good news comes to those who least expect it.

Four Opportunities to Innovate on Innovation

Theologian Donald Kraybill views Jesus' *agape* love as the mark of the upside-down Reign of God.[12] *Agape* inverts our expectations of reality: out is in, down is up, the weak are strong, and the dead are alive. The church "innovates on innovation" by turning the tables on our familiar assumptions about innovation. For example:

"Don't follow your passion."

I'm a big fan of passion. I've written books about it. But advising people to "Follow your passion" and "Do what you love" confuses passion (love worthy of suffering) with bright ideas and enthusiasm, and reduces God's passion (the life, death, and resurrection of Jesus Christ) to self-actualization at best, and self-gratification at worst. Interpreting passion to mean "a thing we were born to do" gets us no further, as the Pixar movie *Soul* delightfully

---

11 Bruggeman, 59.

12 Kraybill, 255.

demonstrates.[13] What's more, most people have no idea
what their "passion" is. William Damon's research at
the Stanford Center for Adolescence found that only one
in five young people between ages of 12 and 26 have a
clear sense of where they want to go, what they want to
accomplish in life, and why.[14]

Complicating our misunderstanding of passion
is the reality of failure – a repeatable rite in every
creative endeavor. It is true that failure is a powerful
form of learning; if we included it in our ministry's
timeline, it would seem far less daunting (especially
if we soften the blow by calling it a "pivot").
Entrepreneurs like to celebrate failure – to "fail fast"
is an important practice in any innovative community.
But Christian social innovators *grieve* failure,
even while recognizing its necessity. Grief helps us
loosen our grip on "our" ideas, and repositions us as
participants in God's "new thing" instead.

Innovating on innovation means exposing false
understandings of passion and offering an alternative.
The church views passion (from the Latin *passio*, "to
suffer" or "to submit") as love worthy of suffering.
True love, after all, is "to die for." This is the passion
God has for us, revealed in the life, death and
resurrection of Jesus Christ, and it is the love God
hopes for in return.[15] Yes, Christian social innovation

---

[13] The story focuses on meek nice guy Joe, part-time middle school band director. See Sonaiya Kelley, "How Pete Docter and Kemp Powers Brought the First Black Pixar Protagonist to Life in 'Soul,'" *The Los Angeles Times* (November 19, 2020), https://www.latimes.com/entertainment-arts/movies/story/2020-11-19/pixar-soul-pete-docter-kemp-powers (accessed April 28, 2021).

[14] See William Damon, *The Path to Purpose: How Young People Find Their Calling in Life* (New York: The Free Press), 2008. Cited in Bill Burnett and Dave Evans, *Designing Your Life* (New York: Knopf, 2016), xxix.

[15] See my book *Practicing Passion: Youth and the Quest for a Passionate Church* (Grand Rapids: Eerdmans), 2004.

97

arises from passion – but if it is Christian social innovation, it gives form to *Christ's* passion, not ours. Christ's passion was not a strategy, but a declaration of love. Following our passion (assuming we can find one) depletes us, but being overcome by Christ's passion makes us new.

"You cannot be anything you want to be."

Despite what advertisers and well-meaning college admissions counselors tell us, "choosing to be anything we want to be" is magical thinking (right up there with "If you build it, they will come"). If we are very lucky, we can choose how to play a few cards we have been dealt, but – thanks be to God – we are not the sum of our choices. Before we are anything else, we are human beings, beloved by God. We did not choose to be human or to be loved, but no choice we makealters these facts. Our humanity is God's gift to us, finitude and all.

Every culture has invented stories to come to grips with human limits—stories that remind us that we have bodies, lifespans and gravity to contend with. Failing to reckon with these limits is the stuff of tragedy. The ancient Greeks told stories about gods who were cursed by limits (Prometheus was chained to a rock for eternity, forced to endure the same brutal day over and over again), and – conversely – about humans who were cursed with immortality (Tithonus was made immortal but not young, and begged for death to overcome him; eventually he became a cicada). All of these stories get at the same basic point: try to be something you're not, and things don't end well.

Yet surprisingly, the very limits that make us human also make us creative. Only God is creatively unconstrained. For the rest of us, "creativity loves constraints," as former Google vice president Marissa Mayer once put it.[16] Human creativity is our most complex, integrative cognitive function; when we must find new solutions to overcome obstacles, every part of the brain pitches in.[17] That is why creating artificial boundaries, like time limits, can make us more creative, not less. At the same time, too much pressure on the imagination always backfires; innovation cannot be manufactured on a schedule or an assembly line. Because innovating for love grows out of our attentiveness to *Who/who*, it requires time for noticing. So, cultivating fallow periods is necessary – seasons when we replenish our water supplies, allow our roots to grow deeper, and above all *pay attention.*

Andrew Root, in his book *The Congregation in a Secular Age,* presents "innovation" as the rationality of Silicon Valley – and he pretty much hates on it every chance he gets.[18] But Root gets a lot of things right, including the dehumanization that results from the acceleration of modern society, which most of us (churches included) fully and unintentionally buy into. Root is deeply concerned with forms of innovation that obliterate, rather than foster, human

[16] The phrase has since attained meme status among designers and social innovators. Cf. Chuck Salter, "Marissa Mayer's 9 Principles of Innovation," *Fast Company* (February 19, 2008), https://www.fastcompany.com/702926/marissa-mayers-9-principles-innovation (accessed July 11, 2021).

[17] See Anna Abraham, "The Neuroscience of Creativity: Q&A with Anna Abraham," *Scientific American* (January 4, 2019), https://blogs.scientificamerican.com/beautiful-minds/the-neuroscience-of-creativity-a-q-a-with-anna-abraham/ (accessed April 29, 2021). Also see Adam Morgan and Mark Barden, *A Beautiful Constraint* (New York: Wiley), 2015. Not all constraints are beautiful, and "they must be balanced with a healthy disregard for the impossible" (former Yahoo CEO Marissa Mayer, cited in Matthew May, "How Intelligent Constraints Drive Creativity," *Harvard Business Review* (January 30, 2013), https://hbr.org/2013/01/how-intelligent-constraints-dr (accessed April 28, 2021).

[18] Andrew Root, *The Congregation in a Secular Age* (Grand Rapids, MI: Baker Press), 2021.

GoodLands
New Haven, CT

Molly Burhans returned to her Catholic faith in college, traveling in Guatemala. She saw how Guatemalan land served as a critical vehicle for food security, ecological stability, and eliminating rural poverty. She made friends who were Christians ("but not the Christians you see on TV – none of the prosperity gospel crap," she said). Burhans experienced them as exactly the opposite: "I began to think, 'Maybe I'm a Christian.'"

Inspired partly by the Catholic Worker Movement and partly by hanging out with "some really cool nuns," Burhans considered joining an order. Instead, she got a master's degree in ecological design. That's when she realized that the Catholic church is one of the world's biggest landowners: convents, art, parishes, cathedrals, farms, forests, oil wells – and two hundred million acres of land. Burhans realized that, at that scale, better land management in the Catholic church alone could make a significant impact on climate change (not to mention refugees, sustainable agriculture, poverty, infrastructure, etc.). She also recognized that, without the church's buy-in, policy changes would have little impact. What if faith could do what science and politics could not?

The problem was, no one had mapped the assets of the Catholic Church – ever. So, Burhans founded GoodLands to help church bodies know what lands they have, so they can reimagine their land use in ways that have the most positive impact on communities and the environment.

Land use has a moral dimension; when GoodLands overlays church lands on geographic information systems (GIS) databases, "high impact sites" become visible – places where small changes in land management can have a big impact on sustainability and justice goals. Burhans prepared the first-ever global data-based map of the Catholic church's presence on earth and took it to the pope. On her first visit, the Swiss Guard led her to a marble hallway in the third loggia of the Apostolic Palace, where huge frescos – maps – adorned the walls. They were commissioned in the early 16th century to depict the world as it was known then. When Burhans asked the guard where the Vatican kept its maps, he pointed to the walls.

After founding GoodLands, Burhans says she spent three years "eating beans and crying." Most of her work, even for the Vatican, was pro bono. (After her first paid project with Catholic schools, things looked up; "I could eat organic beans," she recalls). In 2017, she mapped abuse cases with priests, to prevent abusers from simply "disappearing" into a new assignment. Eventually, she found that abuse cases could be significantly curtailed if the church just focused on five critical episcopal conferences.

As one digital expert put it, "What Molly is trying to do is digitally transform the Catholic Church." (The pope invited her to start the Vatican's first cartography office there, an offer currently in negotiation.) Burhans believes the church could save billions if they embraced her data infrastructure – "As well as improving the world in every single ministry they do...The church's entire financial model [based on morally committed but very cheap labor] does not work with people who need to feed children and send them to school and own a car. That's a moral issue too."

attentiveness – which is very much at risk when we innovate to accomplish more and perform better, instead of innovating for love, which by definition is not self-fulfilling, but self-emptying.

The risk Root identifies is real. We are card-carrying members of a booming cult of busyness designed to overcome, transcend, or ignore human limits. When we get caught up in "doing more faster," which most technical innovations facilitate, we start throwing overboard the parts of our lives that slow us down or limit us: leisure, sabbath, art, compassion, sleep, relationships, neighborhoods, children (Root's beautiful solution to this predicament focuses on children specifically). Tragically, these are the aspects of our lives most deeply connected to our humanity. It turns out that being human, as God created us to be, takes time.

In a famous study conducted at Princeton Seminary in the 1970s, seminarians received a preaching assignment: write a sermon on the parable of the Good Samaritan. The students didn't know they had just been enlisted in an experiment on helping behavior. On the way to the studio where they were to deliver their sermons, some students were told, "You are very late – you need to hurry." Others were told that the professor was "ready" whenever they could get there. Others were told that things weren't quite ready; to "take their time." *En route* to the studio, each student encountered a confederate who appeared destitute and was in obvious "distress." Researchers wanted to know which group of students would be most likely to stop and help. Some 63% of the students in the "low hurry" situation stopped and 45% of the "ready" students stopped. Only 10% of the students who were "running late" stopped. In other words, thinking about the Good Samaritan did not increase helping behavior – but being in a hurry decreased it dramatically.[19]

We all know the sad consequences of "not having time" for such human priorities. Yet if you're like me, you've heard yourself rationalize: "Well, just this once" and "When everything else is done..." (Out of such delusions come songs like Harry Chapin's "Cat's in the Cradle.") When Christian social innovators function as would-be prophets, we remind one another that sacred things slow us down. We cannot be everywhere or everything we want to be. When the church no longer protects human limits, both our humanity and our creativity are at risk.

"You aren't as special as you think."

19   John Darley and Daniel Batson, "From Jerusalem to Jericho: A Study of Situational and Dispositional Variables in Helping Behavior," *Journal of Personality and Social Psychology* 27 (1973), 100-108, https://doi.org/10.1037/h0034449 (accessed April 28, 2021).

Start-ups are legendary for their high failure rate: Twenty percent fail at the end of Year One, 30% after Year Two, 50% after Year Five, and so on, until after Year Ten, only three in 10 are still standing.[20] The most oft-cited statistic is that 90% of start-ups fail – though not until after 15 years. (It's worth noting that a 15-year run for any ministry would generally be heralded as a triumph.) These statistics mask the fact that almost three-fourths of failed first-time entrepreneurs never try again; among those who do try again, success rates improve dramatically, and get higher with each successive try.[21] But there's no way around the basic premise: If you want to start something new, you will need to make peace with failure.[22]

Despite widespread advice advocating innovators to "fail fast" to allow them to improve their ideas faster, it's safe to say that most of us try hard to fail at failure. Others' ideas may not succeed, but (we tell ourselves) we are different. Even as a nation, people in the United States are convinced that we are the exception to the rule. American "exceptionalism" has been on display recently, but the idea that America is called to be a "city on the hill," a light to all nations, has been sewn into our national and religious identity since the Puritans.[23]

---

[20] 2019 StartUp Genome report, cited in Nicolas Cerdeira and Kyril Kotashev, "Start Up Failure Rate: Ultimate Report and Infographic 2021," Failory.com (March 25, 2021), https://www.failory.com/blog/startup-failure-rate (accessed April 30, 2021).

[21] Cited by Allison Schrager, "Failed Entrepreneurs Find More Success the Second Time," *Bloomberg* (July 28, 2014), https://www.bloomberg.com/news/articles/2014-07-28/study-failed-entrepreneurs-find-success-the-second-time-around (accessed April 30, 2021).

[22] The two most common preventable reasons start-ups fail are having the wrong team and failing to research what the customer actually needs before you start. Tom Eisenmann, "Why Start Ups Fail," *Harvard Business Review Magazine* (May- June 2021), httpo://hbr.org/2021/05/why-start-ups-fail (accessed July 11, 2021).

[23] John Winthrop preached his famous "City on a Hill" sermon in 1630. Only in retrospect did this sermon become linked to American exceptionalism. Edward O'Reilly, "John Winthrop's City on a Hill Sermon" and an "Erasure of Collective Memory," *New York Historical Society*

Brueggemann reminds us that this is neither a uniquely American nor modern problem; he compares modern American exceptionalism with ancient Israel's 2,700 years ago.[24] Whenever our sense of "chosenness" runs amuck, we begin to believe that we deserve our blessings because we are special.

Entrepreneurs and innovators are vulnerable to their own brand of exceptionalism. One theory explaining entrepreneurs' high failure rates is the "*hubris* theory of entrepreneurship" – which bears an eerie resemblance to garden-variety sin. The *hubris* theory of entrepreneurship says that many start-ups fail, not because of the start-up, but because of the personalities drawn to entrepreneurship in the first place.[25] Most entrepreneurs have an irrational confidence that their idea is going to work, that their venture will be the unicorn – the one-in-one-hundred longshot that defies the odds. One study revealed that founders overestimate the value of their intellectual property by 255%.[26]

Of course, it does take a certain boldness to take the risks, and to handle the inevitable uncertainties, required for launching a new venture. But the belief that "I'm special" often makes entrepreneurs ignore their limitations, allocate resources poorly and misinterpret data so it "supports" what they want it to say. All of this sets them up to fail. Humility, not *hubris*, is a better predictor of a new venture's success.[27]

(December 5, 2018), https://blog.nyhistory.org/21991-2/ (accessed April 30, 2021).

[24] Brueggemann, *Reality, Grief, Hope,* 24.

[25] Mathew Haward, et al., "A Hubris Theory of Entrepreneurship," *Management Science* 52 (February 1, 2006), 160-172, https://doi.org/10.1287/mnsc.1050.0483 (accessed April 30, 2021).

[26] Cerdeira and Kotashev, n.p.

[27] Steve Tobak, "Hubris Kills Businesses, Humility Saves Them," *Entrepreneur* (October 20, 2015), https://www.entrepreneur.com/article/251811 (accessed April 30, 2021).

In ancient Greece, *hubris* referred to wrongful action against the divine order of the universe – especially ignoring our humanity and believing ourselves to be equal to the gods. *Humility*, on the other hand (from the Latin *humus* – dust or soil – which also gave us the word *human*) refers to an honest appreciation of our gifts, virtues and limits, including where we stand in relationship to God. As we noted earlier, humility is a distinguishing virtue in innovating for love. In Christian social innovation, *God* is the innovator, the giver of new life. Our role is not to work miracles, but to remove the obstacles that prevent people from embracing them. Turning the tables on *hubris* – inverting expectations about power and privilege, whether in the church or society in general – won't make you popular. But trading *hubris* for humility is a sign that we are beginning to embody Christ. How upside-down is our vision for change? Does our ministry turn over any tables? Are the last first? Are the weak empowered? Do the lame walk? If not, we have not innovated on innovation. We have not been innovative enough.

When we place our ideas at Christ's disposal, Christ becomes the hero of the story, not us – which frees us to be the finite characters: the ones who have flaws, make mistakes, take naps and keep Sabbath. If God is the innovator, our perspective shifts from being "the only prophet left in the city" to discerning, naming, blessing and fanning the glimmers of resurrection we see around us – signs that God is already at work in the neighborhood, perhaps even without us. Instead of extracting ourselves from relationships in order to "get stuff done," innovating on innovation means immersing ourselves more deeply into our

Union Coffee
Dallas, TX

Technically a United Methodist church plant, *Union Coffee* originated as a laboratory. It asked: 1) What might a church learn from a neighborhood if it was so embedded there that people actually noticed if they closed? 2) What are alternative means of sustaining good work, beyond the offering plate? 3) What might ministry with young professionals look like who have either left or never engaged the church?

A coffee shop seemed like a good place to start. Since opening in 2012, *Union* has not only become one of Dallas' top independent coffee shops (in Yelp's top 15 in Dallas). It has three worshipping communities, a long list of arts events, and has "kept the city of Dallas awake with more caffeine than we could measure." *Union* resists "reaching" its target audience of young adults. "Nobody wants to be reached," says Community Curator (and pastor) Mike Baughman, "but they do want to be neighbors."

That spirit animates every part of *Union's* identity. Reopened after the pandemic in a new site (it looks like a gracious, large neighborhood home – which it once was), *Union's* first floor is a general coffee shop with ample hang-out space and free WIFI. The second floor has light and airy conference rooms available for rent. *Union* promises "the most generous cup of coffee in town" – and it delivers 10% of profits, plus revenue from fundraisers, go to other nonprofits and area causes. They also give $25,000 a year to a neighboring church's ministry to care for unsheltered neighbors.

"There's been a sad shift in much of the church," says Baughman. "It used to be that a church sat in the middle of a parish – a geographically defined area or neighborhood – and the congregation, along with its assigned priest, were responsible for the overall well-being of the people who lived and worked in the parish. At some point…many churches have become concerned primarily with the spiritual well-being of the people who attend worship on a regular basis. The church has, in large part, abdicated its responsibility to be a good neighbor."

Union sets out to change that. Its commitment to a robust community is especially evident in its storytelling area,

The Naked Stage. "A shared experience of storytelling... breaks down through the vulnerability of the storyteller," Baughman says. *Union* is intentional about becoming a home for young people Baughman describes as "the bored and the burned" – people who have had negative church experiences in the past.

Union Coffee not only aims to change the way churches operate but to change the way businesses operate. "We want to show the world that generosity can be a verdant part of the business world," Baughman says. "The business world wields a mighty stick in our global realities. If a company like Starbucks were to make a commitment like we've made – to only roast fair-trade beans and give back 10% of their revenue to charity – it would transform the lives of millions, and not just the lives of those who pick their beans."

"We may be tilting at windmills," Baughman says, "but I don't know of many organizations who changed the world with mediocre goals."

neighborhoods, attending more fully to others, and de-centering our egos in order to lift up the "new thing" God is doing in our midst.

How to Participate in God's Innovation

It was two weeks before Easter. In late March, in New Jersey, the days still have a cool snap to them. Piles of snow have (mostly) given up and turned to mud; the sun sneaks through the clouds with growing boldness. I was teaching at our school's Farminary (a working farm that doubles as an outdoor classroom) and it was "garden time" – a.k.a., farm chores – which are part of every Farminary class. My group was taking our turn at the compost pile, an eight-foot monstrosity of life-giving stench, which is the most sacred site at the farm. My co-professor Nate Stucky, who oversees the Farminary, never tires of explaining the miracle of the compost pile to students, the way microbes transform decay into life-giving humus, the way God uses compost to challenge our culture's disdain of waste. Everyone works the compost pile, no exceptions, turning leaves and smelly cucumbers into an odd form of hope.

We worked like a swarm of bees, jamming our shovels into the pile to give it some air. Andrea was standing on the top of the pile, boots covered in eggshells and watermelon rinds, when she reeled a little and caught herself. She paused. "I'm sorry," she apologized to her classmates. "I need a minute – I'm a little woozy." And then: "I'm pregnant."

And there it was, the Easter story in a sentence: standing on top of a pile of death came a pronouncement of new life. We stopped to celebrate her nauseous joy.

Now, if I were God – if I had a "big idea" as big as *new life* – I would never start with a compost pile full of goose poop and coffee grounds. I can't fathom how a pile of death can be transformed into life (and plus: *eiew*). I would have gotten a grant, rented the Hilton, hired a band, and had a party: "It's time for new life, everybody! Let's drop the ball!" I would have made The New Life Project the result of a carefully drawn 12-month planning process, had a design sprint and congratulated myself for the excellent team I had assembled. I would be *invested*. I would have "owned" The New Life Project, taken responsibility and, if possible, the credit. I would have poured myself into it, giving it everything I had, and I would have given thanks to God and asked for God's blessing.

I'd be doing it wrong.

Still Waters Landing
Hayesville, NC

One in seven Americans lives in a rural area – described by some sociologists as the "new ghetto" because out-migration, economic hardship, rising crime, and drug abuse have become daily realities. The anger, despair, and resentment seen in crumbling inner cities are now being expressed over the collapse of rural ways of life. Three out of four farmers and farmworkers have been directly impacted by the opioid crisis. Growing rural racial diversity challenges traditional power dynamics. Nearly 90% of "persistent poverty" counties (those with poverty rates above 20% for three decades or more) are rural. And, compared to their urban counterparts, these counties are more likely to remain poor because opportunity programs are scarce in rural areas.

Hayesville, NC (pop. 387) is one such community. Despite stereotypes, rural Americans outside of the Bible Belt are *less* religiously affiliated than their urban cousins. Churches feel this keenly. Six churches serve Hayesville proper, with a dozen more congregations within a 6-mile radius. If three out of five Hayesville residents (the rural U.S. average) go to church, each congregation would have 12.5 people.

Rev. Bryan Wilson serves two of these congregations, Hickory Stand and Oak Forest United Methodist churches. Articulating the needs of his poor community named their reality. But Wilson began to notice assets in the community too – and, as he puts it, "We decided to focus on what we have, not on what we don't have." What rural poor people do have is land – small parcels where agriculture is possible. When two church members offered Wilson the use of their plots – and two friends kicked in two pregnant sows, a boar, and 50 chickens. *Still Waters Landing* was born.

Still Waters Landing is a church without walls, a 10-acre farm that raises vegetables and pasture-raised pigs. Area teenagers serve as farm interns (they get $10 per hour, plus vegetables and a quarter of a pig), and learn life/job skills alongside redemptive agriculture. Many who buy the farm's high-quality pork and produce do not attend church – but Wilson is their pastor, just as he has suddenly become the pastor for restaurant and feed-store owners, local migrant workers, brewers, teachers, school administrators, students, and a local herbalist.

Wilson sees the farm as an especially potent vehicle for young people's discipleship. While *Still Waters Landing's* largest sales contracts come from restaurants, Hayesvillians see the farm as their community space for worship, educational programs, peer-learning days, volunteer opportunities, and well-loved barbecues and music festivals twice a year. As Wilson said, "In a million years, I never thought I'd be doing any of this. But it's the best kind of church I've ever been part of."

Breadcrumbs for Discernment

When we are part of God's innovation, we don't pour our lives out through our work; God uses our lives to pour divine life into creation, into us and through us. When God is the innovator, the rules of our expected reality change. Power is upside-down. The poor inherit the earth and the hungry are satisfied, the weeping laugh and those who suffer for Christ are exalted (Luke 6:20-22). God's innovation is the embodiment of love, *agape* – and the measurable outcome is new life.

When I work with people sorting through new ideas for ministry – or new life directions (they often go together) – I often use an exercise I learned from one of my Ministry Incubator colleagues, Werner Ramirez, Associate Pastor of Fifth Avenue Presbyterian Church in New York City. Despite his urban location, Werner is a garden geek; during his seminary days he logged countless hours on the Farminary compost pile. Werner's favorite discernment exercise is to compost ideas. He asks people to write down (one idea per sticky note, in good design fashion) every idea that energizes them. And then he takes people to a compost pile – a real one, if he can find one – gives them a shovel, and asks them to compost every idea except one. His point is that just because we must let go of a hunch – or a hope, or life trajectory – does not mean God is finished with it. Maybe the idea needs time to germinate, or maybe it is incomplete on its own, or maybe it needs to decompose a little and recombine with some other nutrients. Maybe it is the right course of action for someone, but not for you. In the compost pile, those discarded ideas are transformed into something life-giving. Not by us, but by God.

How do we know that we are participating in God's innovation instead of co-opting God into ours? The quick answer is: we don't. Aligning our vision with God's vision is not as simple as checking a box; it is an ongoing, communal practice of discernment that connects dozens of tiny clues. The life of faith is more about following breadcrumbs than blueprints, but here are a few principles that guide people who innovate for love:

1. **Who before Why**
2. **Awe before Excellence**
3. **Humility before Hero**
4. **Abundance, not Scarcity**

Figure 4.1

Guiding Principles for Christian Social Innovators

1. Who before Why

As we have already noted, people who innovate for love start with *who*. If you were ever giddily smitten by the kid sitting behind you in algebra (not that I know about this), you remember how love precedes reason. Love will break your heart – that is what makes it love – and grief is uninterested in *why*. Grief always points to *who*. Christian social innovation is fundamentally local; it begins with paying attention to people in our "orbit" (families, neighborhoods, spheres of interaction) whose suffering we are compelled to address. We connect to their pain and share in their grief. Attention, as French mystic Simone Weil reminded us, is a form of prayer, which means paying attention is the first step in discerning God's direction.[28] Your personal connection to the people you hope to bless is precious and rare and singular. Through your *who*, your *why* emerges.

2. Awe before Excellence

Innovating for love shifts our metrics, as well. Specifically, Christian social innovation aims for awe, not excellence. Stuck as we are in a performance culture, the abstract standard of "excellence" spells trouble for innovators, pitting virtuosos against explorers, the need to impress against the need to experiment, risk, fail, pivot, and try again.

In Christian Scripture, many Greek terms are translated into the English word *excellent*, but most of them refer to moral virtues; the "excellent way," for Paul, is love (I Cor. 12:31). Christians are called to "excel in love" (I Cor. 8:7); all other excellences flow from this. Safe to say that our contemporary understanding of "excellence" as "double-plus good"[29] was not on Paul's mind when he dictated his letters to his scribes. God cares that we love well – and is little interested in how well we perform. That does not mean we should be slouches at innovation, or anything else, but it gives us permission to make a mess as we learn the art of unbinding.

Awe has no goal of excellence; it has no goal at all. Awe *beholds*. Awe takes the rug out from under

---

[28]   Simone Weil, *Gravity and Grace,* trans. Emma Craufurd, (London: Routledge and Kegan Paul), 1952. Excerpt at https://rohandrape.net/ut/rttcc-text/Weil1952d.pdf (accessed May 1, 2021).

[29]   Haidt, Jonathan. *The Happiness Hypothesis: Finding Modern Truth in Ancient Wisdom.* (New York: Basic Books, 2006), 203.

us and makes us small before a mystery that leaves us both trembling and energized.[30] Christian social innovators know the feeling well: What if I don't know what I'm doing? What if God wants me to do it anyway? Standing near God's overwhelming greatness makes us look silly, not excellent; it leaves us barefoot and blubbering (Moses) or speechless and humbled (Zachariah). In awe, we are the opposite of excellent; we are momentarily useless – which is the point. Theology without awe *is* useless; awe is the "beginning of wisdom" (Prov. 9:10). Christian social innovation inevitably has impact goals and outcomes to report – but the ministry objective is awe, not effectiveness. Awe is the result of the figure-ground shift that happens when we stand at the foot of the cross, and suddenly recognize the crucified Christ for who He is. We can do nothing from this position except behold and share the centurion's dumbfounded confession: "Truly this man was the Son of God!" (Mark 15:39).

3. Humility before Hero

In Greta Gerwig's coming-of-age movie *Ladybird*, Saoirse Ronan plays 16-year-old Ladybird (she says Ladybird is her given name, as in: "I gave it to myself"). Ladybird is a bored, so-so student who explores a number of ways to come into her own.

"What I'd really like," she tells the school counselor tentatively, "is to be on Math Olympiad."

Sister Sarah is direct: "But math isn't something you're terribly strong in…"

Ladybird finishes the sentence for her: "…*that we know of.* Yet."

---

[30] See Rudolph Otto, *The Idea of the Holy* (Oxford, UK: Oxford University Press), 1958.

The scene is a spot-on portrayal of what Stanford psychologist Carol Dweck calls a "growth mindset" – the idea that human capacity is not predetermined or cast in stone, but can be cultivated. Dweck lifts up the example of a teacher who, instead of failing students whose work was not up to snuff, gave them the grade *"Not Yet."* In a growth mindset, Dweck writes, "Failure can be a painful experience. But it doesn't define you. It's a problem to be faced, dealt with, and learned from."[31]

One of the gifts humility offers Christian social innovators is a growth mindset. Participating in God's "new thing" means losing the hero mentality fast, shunning both its savior connotations (My idea will change the world!) and its martyr complex when things go wrong (I am all alone!) The hero innovates on her own steam. Innovators for love, on the other hand, secure in the knowledge that bodies, time limits, and the need for sleep are God's gifts to us. So they open themselves both to the divine energy found through the spiritual resources of Christian tradition (e.g., prayer, liturgy, Sabbath, sacraments, searching Scripture, gratitude, etc.) and to the shared energy of the Christian community (e.g., encouraging friends and mentors, conversation, relevant expertise). At its best, innovating for love restores us more than it depletes us.

4. Abundance, Not Scarcity

Christian social innovators steward abundance rather than manage scarcity. Not every economic decision involves money (sharing economies, for

[31] Carol Dweck, Mindset: *The New Psychology of Success* (New York: Ballentine Books, 2007) 256.

instance, trade goods for services), but at some point a money conversation is necessary. Sustainability is a topic I have not addressed adequately in these pages, simply because it could be a book of its own. But mission-aligned financial plans and practices are important markers that distinguish Christian social innovator from others. Given the collapse of traditional revenue streams for many churches, it is imperative that Christian social innovators have some "real talk" about money – especially because sustainability is the fruit of a theology of abundance, not assumed scarcity.

People in ministry regularly shoot themselves in the foot when it comes to revenue models, mostly because we do not like the idea of having one. We have our reasons. Compared to charity, which is our dominant paradigm for church economics, a self-sustaining financial model somehow feels selfish. "If we are part of God's 'new thing,'" we tell ourselves, "we should just offer our services *pro bono*." Sometimes we adopt a purity mindset: the economic system is broken and participating in it would betray our conscience and prop up a corrupt system. Sometimes we treat money as the "Necessary Evil" to ministry's "Inherent Goodness," or we fail to see the inherent connection between money and ministry. We forget that churches have financial models too; they just don't work very well. And when a church's financial model fails, the church closes.

Space does not permit a thorough discussion of these points, but we can confidently say this much: innovating for love requires a mindset of abundance, not scarcity. Scarcity tends to dominate modern financial thinking; the shift to an abundance mindset is as much a creative challenge as a financial one. Yet innovating for love *requires* an economy of abundance; God calls us to steward waterfalls, not ration drinks in a drought. This requires a change in fundraising strategies, for we have a moral obligation to provide responsible financial support to workers, without fleecing clients or resorting to "magical thinking" about support from church budgets (unlikely) or grants (less likely).

It may be less daunting than we think; after all, we have been here before. When religion in the United States stopped receiving tax support in the early 1800s, churches panicked, and scrambled to find new forms of fiscal support. For the next 50 years, they innovated: passing around alms boxes, subscriptions, pew rentals, tithes, membership fees, "mother-daughter churches," even "taxing" members. Some Southern churches had the horrific practice of holding lands and slaves (and their offspring) to rent out to area farmers.[32] Not until the late 1800s did crowdsourcing – i.e., free will offerings – become commonplace. As Mark Elsdon reminds us, congregations have more assets than they realize, which can be used in ways that either support or compromise our mission.[33] What we lack is an imagination about how to use those assets for ministry – especially ministries that move beyond the expected activities in a church building.

In recent decades, shifting patterns in philanthropy (including giving to church-based ministries) have received enormous attention. We too are in a period of financial experimentation. Asset redeployment (e.g., using church lands, buildings, savings and other holdings differently), new economic practices (e.g., denominational foundations that invest in ministry

---

32   James Hudnut-Beumler, *In Pursuit of the Almighty's Dollar: A History of Money and American Protestantism* (Chapel Hill, NC: University of North Carolina Press, 2007), 8-9.

33   Mark Elsdon, *We Aren't Broke* (Grand Rapids: Eerdmans), 2021.

start-ups instead of Amazon, impact investing, circular and sharing economies), philanthropic innovation (angel philanthropy, donor-advised investing, etc.) and "mixed economy" revenue models that combine private and public forms of funding are all finding new hearings in churches. These experiments challenge the dominant "charity mindset" of congregations. The goal is to find new financial practices that are life-giving to all parties, and that erase distinctions between giver and recipient, "haves" and "have nots," server and servant.[34]

Find Your Calcutta

Christian activist Shane Claiborne often tells the story of traveling to India to work with Mother Teresa and the Sisters of Charity, hoping to find "an old nun who believed Jesus meant what he said."[35] "Mother," as she was called in the streets, was hard to pin down; it took Shane awhile to get an audience with her. When he finally got one, he was so overwhelmed that he couldn't think of anything to say. He wanted a hug. She gave it to him. She told him what she told everybody: "Calcuttas are everywhere if we only have eyes to see. Find your Calcutta." Claiborne knew it was time to come home.

Claiborne is best known for founding *The Simple Way*, an intentional community in Philadelphia committed to ending poverty – although Claiborne himself has been an evangelist for many causes, most recently ending gun violence. Claiborne and Mike Martin, a

---

[34] Charity is critical in times of crisis, but over long periods of time can force demoralizing patterns of dependency onto beneficiaries. Research on the negative impact of charity vast and consistent; for a basic introduction to both problems and solutions, see Robert Lupton's *Toxic Charity* (San Francisco: HarperOne), 2012 and *Charity Detox* (San Francisco: HarperOne), 2016.

[35] Shane Claiborne, *The Irresistible Revolution: Living as an Ordinary Radical* (Grand Rapids: Zondervan, 2006), 78.

youth minister-turned-blacksmith, recently toured
the country, promoting a book they co-wrote after yet
another round of school shootings.[36] At each stop they
held a rally (more like a revival) on gun reform. Martin
set up his forge and anvil at every venue, and literally
beat a sword – in this case, a donated gun that had been
used in a violent crime – into a garden tool.

I met Martin a year before the tour, when I took a
group of seminarians to his backyard forge in Colorado
Springs. He taught us to make a garden rake from a
gun with a story (we donated our awkward-looking
tool to the Farminary when we returned to campus).
After the murders at Sandy Hook Elementary School in
2012, Martin had felt called to respond. He hung up his
youth minister hat and entered the world of Christian
social innovation. He didn't set out to be a social
innovator; he set out to find a creative way to embody
a prophetic imagination toward gun violence. So, he
trained to become a blacksmith and founded RawTools,
a nonprofit (now in partnership with The Mennonite
Church, U.S.A.) that, in addition to making garden
tools out of guns used in violent crimes, offers training,
resources, and networking around gun reduction and
nonviolence.[37]

This is Mike Martin's Calcutta. Martin is as
unassuming as they come. He is the opposite of the
hero-preneur. His *why* is his *who*: his heart breaks
for the victims of gun violence, and his love for Jesus
compels him to respond. Martin knows the story of

---

[36] Shane Claiborne and Mike Martin, *Beating Guns: Hope for People Who Are Weary of Violence* (Ada, MI:Brazos Press), 2019.

[37] https://rawtools.org Products made from guns used in violent crimes are available for sale on the website, though RawTools' primary funding comes through partnerships and donations.

every gun given to him. He has heard the stories of hundreds of shattered lives and has witnessed small glimmers of redemption when someone hands him "the gun," knowing that it will now and forever be an instrument of peace. Excellence is not the point (though his work looked excellent to me). Martin's ministry is a study in reverence: he aims to wake people up by creating space for the prophet's task of grief. He is a quiet furnace of passion, driven to "forge peace and disarm hearts," as the RawTools website declares, until there is war no more.

He innovates for love.

Conversations

- What is your group or Expedition team's Calcutta?

- Which new ministry ideas does your team need to compost? Which one still has the most energy?

- What problems/realities do you need to name—and grieve – before describing an alternative future? How much denial or resistance will you face when you name those realities?

- What about "innovating on innovation" (pp. 96-98) appeals to you? Which piece of upside-down advice do you find yourself resisting?

- Where do you see signs of "innovating for love" (Figure 4.1, p. 111) in your group's idea for ministry?

What Next?

- As your group or Expedition team zeros in an idea, complete "Chasing God's Dream" and "Mission Mad Libs" on pp. 161-165.

CHAPTER FIVE
Why Do This?

In 1909, the American blacksmith's union experienced a dip in their membership. So, *The Blacksmith's Journal* – hoping to ensure an adequate supply of blacksmiths for a nation on the move – printed an appeal, urging every member of the blacksmith trade to secure at least one additional recruit for the union. America's blacksmiths responded like champs, and in 1910, membership in the blacksmith's union rose.[1] Yet within a decade, the blacksmith's trade had all but died out. The reason, of course, was that in 1908, Henry Ford began mass production of the Model-T. By 1910, he was manufacturing affordable tractors. The world still needed ironworkers, but the industrial landscape in the United States was changing, which meant blacksmiths had to expand their imaginations.

It's possible that today's churches produce better blacksmiths than at any time in history: in many ways, our ministries have never been better. Congregational leaders in previous eras could never have imagined the range of ways we support ministry today:

---

[1] *The Blacksmith's Journal,* vol. 10 (March, 1909), 11. The call was re-issued with biblical zeal the next October: "If every blacksmith would secure one new member to the fold during the coming year, what a mighty organization this would be. And yet we have a few members who secure from one to fifty. Go thou and do likewise" (vol. 10, [October 1909], 18). https://www. google.com/books/edition/_/pBSjAAAAMAAJ?hl=en&gbpv=1 (accessed April 29, 2021).

workshops, training programs, educational resources, organizations, books, and websites (not to mention formal theological education). Church leaders are better educated, better resourced and better networked than ever before. The problem, of course, is that our *context* for ministry has changed. Change has found us. Now the question is not *"Will* we innovate?" but *how*: "Will we innovate for love or for something else?" We stand on an unknown shoreline. What would make the church make sense to people here on Malta? Ironworkers are necessary, but no one has shod a horse in decades.

There's more to the blacksmith analogy. When the blacksmith trade collapsed a century ago, blacksmiths did not simply disappear. They became the nation's first mechanics and welders. By 1920, *The Blacksmith's Journal* – still in print – urged union members to find work in shipbuilding, an ascendant industry in the United States, where metalsmiths were needed.[2] Blacksmiths learned to ply their trade in new ways, with new products: in the heartland, they became boilermakers and machinists for railroads and factories; on the coasts, they took jobs as welders in shipyards. True, trade journals record a period of disorientation. Experienced blacksmiths fervently clung to their identities as craftsmen, not laborers; they resisted rebranding as machinists and welders (thanks to new technologies, young people entering those new trades needed far less preparation and experience than the long-apprenticed blacksmith had received; blacksmiths commonly viewed these youngsters as hacks). In 1949, American blacksmiths finally voted to join the Boilermaker union. Interestingly, today's boilermakers

---

[2]   Sir Francis Henderson, "Shipbuilding in America," *The Blacksmith's Journal* 22 (January 1920), 1-2. https://www.google.com/books/edition/_/vqGjAAAAMAAJ?hl=en&gbpv=1 (accessed April 29, 2021).

are experiencing their own industry disruptions, and are calling on their members to innovate.[3]

If they can do it, so can we.

Why Do This?

I still get quizzical looks when people who know me learn that I have spent the last decade teaching spiritual entrepreneurship and social innovation, among other things, and working with churches, individuals, and especially young people who are looking for new ways to live out their Christian callings.

I am a little shocked to find myself here as well; it has been a steep learning curve. Like most ministers, I am trained as a pastor and an academic, not a social entrepreneur. Most people involved with Christian social innovation (so far) didn't plan to be here, myself included; my primary work is still with adolescents and young adults in churches – except that, increasingly, these young people are not *in* churches. More and more, ministry with young people means finding young people where they live and work, embedding the church beside them as seek meaning, purpose, and belonging (which churches promise, but often fail to deliver) in other domains like sustainable agriculture, health and wellness, placemaking and community development, and creative arts, to name a few. These spaces welcome experimentation, and most have cobbled together traditions, patron saints, and special stories of their own. They incubate their own forms of social innovation that, interestingly, quite often have spiritual dimensions, in practice if not in name. Young people

3 Cf. Newton Jones, "For Boilermakers, Resilience Is Not Unprecedented," *Boilermaker Reporter* 60 (January-March 2021), https://boilermakers.org/news/commentary/v60n1/for-boilermakers-resilience-is-not-unprecedented (accessed April 29, 2021).

often say these domains give them identity and purpose that feel vaguely sacred, if not Christian.

To a catechized imagination, it is easy to see Christ is at work in these spaces, though He often goes unnamed and unnoticed. But because the church is overwhelmingly absent from these domains beyond congregations, faith is mostly on mute. There are notable exceptions (see *Nuns and Nones, p. 25)*, but for the most part no one is building bridges that connect these innovators' stories with the church's Story. That means there is no way of letting innovators know that the church, the people who participate in God's innovation, experience their work, their gifts, and their lives almost sacramentally, as material expressions of God's grace.

I wound up in social innovation because I chased young people here. I was just trying to keep up with them, when one day I lifted my head and looked around, and here I was. Seven in 10 young adults work to create positive social change on a daily basis, according to a 2020 YMCA/OnePoll survey.[4] Significantly, they are not merely looking for productive forms of service. For young adults especially, creating change is a meaning-making activity, a creative outlet, which often offers purposeful community and something akin to mystical or sacred alignment. In short, social innovation very often has spiritual significance for young people – with or without an accompanying religious story. Meanwhile, studies consistently show that young Americans trust small business to improve society more than they trust NGOs, religion, government, or social media.[5] In short,

[4]   "Young Americans Optimistic about Creating Change, Survey Finds," *Philanthropy News Digest* (November 29, 2019), https://philanthropynewsdigest.org/news/young-americans-op-timistic-about-creating-change-survey-finds (accessed April 28, 2021).

[5]   For reasons unexplained, worldwide trust in business in general plummeted after 2018, falling

Nuns and Nones
Building Sacred Bridges

"These are radical, badass women," said Sarah Jane Bradley – a spiritual-but-not-religious single 30-something, describing her roommates: octogenarian Roman Catholic sisters. "[They] have lived lives devoted to social justice, and we can learn from them."

Nuns and Nones started as a six-month experiment and became a national movement. Protestant pastor Wayne Muller and Jewish activist Adam Horowitz, a 32-year-old community organizer, knew many young adults who wanted to live their lives wholly committed to justice and community transformation, but they were broke, overworked, and isolated. Muller, meanwhile, was concerned about these idealistic millennials' burnout rate. He wanted to find some role models who could show them how to live idealistic lives sustainably.

Enter the nuns. After a few daylong seminars that brought together "nuns and nones," they decided to move in together.

There are concrete benefits for both parties. Millennial men and women receive cheap lodging in the convent in return for helping care for the sisters. The sisters – who typically live in huge convents built for a different era – get some income for upkeep. (The average age of a Catholic sister in the U.S. is 80).

But participants bristle at the idea that *Nuns and Nones* is primarily a housing arrangement. The nones ask about the sisters' vows, spiritual practices, rituals; they join convent activities (and sometimes Mass) and share in meals and Bible studies. In return, sisters join millennials for things like Shabbat, dances, and the occasional protest. They often find surprising common ground (a life of chastity turned out to be especially appealing to millennials in the pilot group).

Both parties see it as a "mutual ministry." One sister said, "We have been looking at how to get more connected with the younger generation – and here they were, dropped in our present space, saying, 'We want to learn from you.' It really did blow my mind."

Horowitz calls *Nuns and Nones* a "moral laboratory." "It has totally rocked my world," he admits. "[It's] been one of the strongest senses of flow and calling I've ever experienced." Fellow founder, millennial Katie Gordon, is more direct: "The spirit-led nature of this initiative feels undeniable."

young adults hoping to "make a difference" in the world are much more likely to become entrepreneurs than public servants or church workers.

I decided that if youth thought social innovation was a more trustworthy route to an alternative vision for humanity than the church, I needed to understand why.

Ministry by Any Other Name

Now that entertainment models of youth ministry in church basements have largely run their course, Christian social innovation has become a common alternative context for ministry with young people. That is noteworthy, since from its inception youth ministry has reliably served as the church's research and development department, and tends to foreshadow trends to come. A few years ago, I was speaking at a large youth ministry conference in England, talking about youth in churches, when a young woman cornered me on a break. "Why are you always talking about 'the church?'" she asked. "Youth aren't in the church."

Suddenly I remembered where I was. As much as Americans gripe about our dwindling church attendance, our membership statistics would make European Christians weep for joy. The young woman was right, at least about England: only 1% of British young adults attend the Church of England, and 70% of British young people say they have no religion at all.[6] It suddenly dawned on me that the youth in the United States were headed in a similar direction. (The

from around 70% to 55%. Information from 2020 Edelman Trust Barometer and *Deloitte Global Millennial Survey* 2020, file:///Users/kenda.dean/Downloads/Deloitte_Global_Millennial_Survey_2020.pdf (accessed April 28 2021).

6   Harriet Sherwood, "Less than Half of Britons Expected to Tick 'Christian' in UK Census," *The Guardian* (March 20, 2021), https://www.theguardian.com/world/2018/sep/07/church-in-crisis-as-only-2-of-young-adults-identify-as-c-of-e (accessed April 27, 2021).

statistics are not parallel, but in the United States 63% of teenagers say they are Christian and 36% of millennials say they belong to a church, mosque, or synagogue. One in three say they have no religion in particular.)[7]

Nonetheless, I was speaking at a *youth ministry* conference with more than 1,000 youth workers; who *were* all these people, if they weren't working in churches? I began to pay attention to people's name tags. I met pastors, of course, but also teachers, a wrestling coach, YMCA staff, community youth workers, parachurch youth leaders, university students, social workers, denominational staff, volunteers with sports leagues and hunger programs and theatre troupes. All these people saw themselves as youth ministers, yet "youth ministry" was not in their job description.

Youth ministry in the United Kingdom seemed to have turned "inside out." These youth ministers were not focused primarily on churchgoers or people "attracted" to congregations; their ministries were focused on the lives of young people in neighborhoods, schools, health clinics, community organizations. The number of young people who need Christ in the U.K. hadn't changed; the need for youth ministers was as high as ever. What changed was where those young people were found. Youth ministers seemed to be *deployed* by the church more than employed by the church. Someone in England had had the presence of mind – even as churches closed their doors – to acknowledge that being a youth minister does not

[7] "Religious Affiliation Among American Adolescents," Pew Research Center (September 10, 2020), https://www.pewforum.org/2020/09/10/religious-affiliation-among-american-adolecocnts/, Gallup statistics cited by Scott Neuman, "Fewer Than Half of U.S. Adults Belong to a Religious Congregation," NPR.org (March 30, 2021), https://www.npr.org/2021/03/30/982671783/fewer-than-half-of-u-s-adults-belong-to-a-religious-congregation-new-poll-shows (both accessed April 27, 2021).

depend on who employs us. It depends on *who we love.*

Learning to See the Gorilla: *Schotomas* and Hope

I did not plan to spend so many years teaching faith communities how to expand their imaginations for ministry. The reason I stayed at it is *hope.* Years ago, I taught a continuing education seminar with Mark Devries (my dear friend and co-founder of Ministry Incubators – though at the time that idea had not yet occurred to us). The seminar was on youth ministry, entrepreneurship, and social innovation, and the participants were a bunch of dispirited youth pastors. The economy had tanked; the youth ministry "profession" was beginning its decade-long crumble. Churches bled youth ministry jobs. People who had spent years training to focus their ministries on young people suddenly had no place to go.

It would have been easy to reduce the problem to money. Cash flow was clearly an issue. Small immigrant congregations were overflowing with young people but had no money for staff to pastor them. Large congregations with full staff found their coffers and youth rosters decimated and eliminated age-level ministry positions. Mid-sized congregations that had once supported two pastors were down to one, with youth ministry falling to no one in particular. The era of the professional youth minister had come to an end.

But there was more to the story. These youth workers labored in congregations that shared a *schotoma* – a blind spot, an ability to view an entire landscape while missing something right under their noses. The shifts churches were experiencing had been predicted and discussed for decades. But when it came time to create new ways to connect the gospel with young people, congregations were stymied. They could not imagine ministry apart from their old educational and economic models. Alternative forms of youth ministry (including ministries that jettisoned youth groups altogether) and new ways to fund leadership were available, but since they did not "fit" people's expectations for churches, they were overlooked. It was not that churches were unwilling to consider them; they just had no mental categories to put them in. They didn't *see* them.

A *schotoma* is a real condition of the eye, but it's also a term psychologists use to describe how we make sense of reality: we inadvertently ignore things that don't fit. You may remember a famous experiment in 1999 in which researchers asked people if they thought they would notice if a gorilla walked through a basketball game.[8] Nine out of ten people said yes, of course they would notice. Then the researchers showed a short video of people playing a pick-up game of basketball, and asked participants to count how many times the ball was passed. About thirty seconds into the video, a woman wearing a gorilla suit walked through the basketball game, stopped in the middle of the action, and thumped her chest, and walked on. After watching the video, researchers asked how many people saw the gorilla. Almost half said, "What gorilla?"[9]

On the one hand, *schotomas* help us focus; they act

---

[8] See the video here: https://www.youtube.com/watch?v=vJG698U2Mvo.

[9] The study was repeated in 2010, with different distractions, but the number of people with "unintentional blindness" remained consistent. See Daniel Simons, "But Did You See the Gorilla? The Problem with Unintentional Blindness," *Smithsonian Magazine* (September 2012), https://www.smithsonianmag.com/science-nature/but-did-you-see-the-gorilla-the-problem-with-inattentional-blindness-17339778/ (accessed July 13, 2021).

as invisibility cloaks that shield us from extraneous information. If you're counting passes in a basketball game, an inconvenient gorilla just gets in the way – so we screen it out. On the other hand, these blind spots make it very difficult to entertain genuinely new ideas and imagine alternatives to our present reality. The problem was not that churches resisted new forms of youth ministry; the problem was that they couldn't see them.

Back to the con ed event. Mark and I invited the youth workers to think about ways they could love young people outside the context of a formal youth ministry program, in ways that did not require financial support from their church. Almost everyone had a "hunch" shoved in the back of their minds. Given a little air and conversation, those hunches blossomed into ideas, and then into plans. Over the course of three days, we saw something happen in the room that we have now seen again and again. People named what they saw happening. They grieved together, often with tears. And somehow those tears watered seeds of hope that, by the last session, came roaring to life. One participant told us, "When I came here, I thought I was going to have to leave youth ministry. Now I see that God is just calling me to return home by a different way."

It's hard to turn your back on hope.

Mark and I redesigned a second seminar, thinking it would be our last. Neither of us have time for these things. But hope kept coming, washing over weary church leaders like rain after a drought, refreshing them. You could watch it happen. Anyone who has been part of a ministry incubator – and there are hundreds of them now – has seen this phenomenon. People left these events (we eventually called them "hatchathons") having watched the seedling they

Try Pie Bakery
Waterloo, Iowa

"Know what the Cedar Valley needs? It needs pie, homemade pie."

Waterloo teenager

That was the statement that led to the birth of *Try Pie Bakery* in the Spring of 2014, a nonprofit teen employment program that gives young women from across the socio-economic spectrum, from diverse cultural backgrounds, their first job opportunity. Girls work between 7-12 hours each week and are mentored by volunteers.

It's more than this, of course. *Try Pie* calls itself a "social enterprise-structured youth ministry," born out of a partnership between two congregations from different parts of a divided community. *Try Pie* teaches teens to manage their paychecks, develop basic life skills, understand their unique gifts, and recognize the value in each other. In addition to baking pies (more than 1,000 per week, counting mini pies), *Try Pie* immerses teenagers in its four core values: financial stewardship, job-skill development, faith development, and reconciling community. And of course, laughter – lots of laughter.

Try Pie emerged after Orchard Hill and Harvest Vineyard churches spent many months working together to get to know the youth in the Walnut neighborhood of Waterloo. They asked teenagers for ideas to improve life in their neighborhood, and the needs were many: teen employment, positive activities, racial reconciliation, a caring community for girls – all were necessary.

That's when one young woman said: "What we need is pie." So, a pie bakery was born.

Try Pie started in the church kitchen and the girls sold pies at their churches after worship. Today, *Try Pie* operates as a brick-and-mortar store, has expanded its menu to include (pie shakes!) and recently launched a food truck. *Try Pie* insists on helping teenagers see their work as an outgrowth of faith in Christ. Girls "gain employment experience and get paid," says *Try Pie* director Megan Tensen, "but they also learn core values and build friendships with girls they work with."

came with grow into a cornstalk, ready to love people in new ways that had real traction in their communities. These spiritual entrepreneurs buoyed one another up: *Gastrochurch* in Houston, *Burning Bush Brewery* in Chicago, *Columbia Future Forge* in Washington, the *Brain Kitchen* in Indiana, the *Farminary* at Princeton Seminary (to name a few). Some flourished (see *Try Pie; inset*); some were penguins (see *The Feed Truck, p. 175*).

Our Elijah-complexes are embarrassingly easy to activate ("I'm the only one!"), but when people with the smallest inkling of an idea for an unconventional ministry find others who are similarly wired, the floodgates open. A little permission, as it turns out, goes a long way. We have long known the benefits of vocational friendships for health (and longevity) in ministry, but it turns out these connections are also vital for Christian social innovators.[10] As it turned out, hatchathons mostly hatched *hope,* with some new ministries in its wake. In the company of strangers, people became prophets, standing in the gap between critique and possibility. They beheld God's mystery in one another, which left them both trembling and energized. They had a new confidence that God was afoot. They were agog that God had invited them – *them!* – to be part of a "new thing" God was doing.

The only question was: what must happen next?

---

[10] David Wood is among those who have interpreted some of this research for faith leaders, especially the recovery of friendship in the church as a form of love; see "The Recovery and Promise of Friendship," Princeton Lectures on Youth, Church and Culture 28 (Princeton, NJ: Princeton Theological Seminary, 2007), 165-180. For a more recent take on the importance of holy friendship, see Victoria Atkinson White, "The Gift of Friends Who Challenge Our Sin," *Faith and Leadership* (March 5, 2019), https://faithandleadership.com/victoria-atkinson-white-gift-friends-who-challenge-our-sin; "Institutional Fragility Calls for Holy Friendships," *Faith and Leadership* (June 11, 2019), https://faithandleadership.com/victoria-atkinson-white-institutional-fragility-calls-holy-friendships (both accessed May 1, 2021).

The Work Left to Do: Getting Beyond Starfish Ministries

It is important to admit we are at the thin end of the wedge when it comes to ministry on Malta. As you have noticed from the examples offered in this book, most "innovative" ministries aren't all that new when we consider the scope of Christian history, even though they are new to us. Christian social innovators need not join the cult of originality; we do not aim for originality – we aim for the boldness to imitate Christ. Participating in God's "new thing" is always more about our love than our ideas: God's innovation in Jesus Christ has already happened, and every ministry we create merely echoes the life-giving, upside-down work that God has already started. The question to ask is not how innovative our ministries are, but can we be accused of "turning the world upside down" (Acts 17:6) with the love of Jesus? Creating a theological framework for Christian social innovation is still in its early stages, but this work remains critical so that our innovation genuinely reflects the table-turning love of Jesus Christ.

Second, so far, most of the ministries launched in the name of Christian social innovation have been "starfish" ministries. I'm referring to that old story about the man walking along a beach full of washed-up starfish, who saw an old fisherman hurling one starfish at a time back into the surf. The man commented on the futility of the fisherman's efforts. "Why do you bother?" he asked the fisherman. "Look at all these starfish – throwing back one or two isn't going to matter." The fisherman picked up another starfish and threw it into the sea, saying simply: "It mattered to that one."

We can't unbind everyone. Instead of being overwhelmed by the enormity of need around us,

Christian social innovators tend to manage expectations by noting how transformative our work has been to a few starfish, a select group of people whose lives were truly turned upside down because they encountered Christ's love through a particular ministry. The trade-off is that the overall impact of these ministries remains quite small; they are more outposts than nerve centers for Jesus. To be clear, Jesus is not counting starfish; one transformed life, one lost sheep, is worth going after, for God and for us. The grace of Christ that lobbed us gasping starfish back into the sea is lavish and wasteful, and ministry inevitably is the same.

At the same time, few social innovations outlast their founders and without pastoral support, Christian social innovators seldom wield enough power in ecclesial systems to gain much traction, support, and visibility in the larger church. In some ways, this is the nature of ministry: it is necessarily locally defined and focused on specific needs of specific neighborhoods and communities.

Thinking Bigger: Why Systems Matter

But Christians are not only called to apply salve to wounds; we are also called to change the systems that cause these wounds in the first place. Shaping a society from below is a long game, and starfish inevitably wash up onshore faster than we can throw them back. What remains to be done is for Christians to apply our innovative imaginations to systems as well as to individual ministries. Human needs like housing, health care, employment, child care, and education (to name a few) have inspired heroic innovations from individuals and some congregations, but widespread cooperation between faith communities around systemic innovation has not yet captured our ecclesial imaginations. Problems like immigration, climate change, food waste, racism, human trafficking, substance abuse (the list goes on) all have been addressed by passionate innovators—but innovating for love at scale is a long way off.

Meanwhile, efforts to align innovation and assets, money and mission, are gathering momentum—but they are still largely disconnected conversations. Church closures and sales of religious properties continue to accelerate, with potentially devastating consequences.[11] The National Trust of Canada estimates that one-third of Canada's faith buildings are in danger of closing in the next decade, displacing not only worshipping communities, but day care centers, women and seniors' programs, arts and culture organizations, twelve-step groups, food banks, blood donor clinics, and countless other community activities that cannot pay commercial rental rates.

On the surface, this scenario sounds like a minor cultural inconvenience, not an international crisis. Yet small "mediating groups," such as those offered by religious communities, are the primary ways human communities forge trust and inspire cooperation. Mediating communities build bridges between diverse groups of people who come together to construct a common story. When mediating groups vanish, these bridges disintegrate, along with trust and a sense

---

[11] Economic development consultant Rick Reinhard predicts that the next several years will see the closing of as many as 100,000 houses of worship throughout the United States, "up from an estimated 3,750 to 8,000 per year now. While it is easy to blame COVID-19 for the upcoming closings, most of the churches were on the brink of shuttering pre-pandemic." Rick Reinhard, "A Call to Re-examine United Methodist Real Estate," *UMNews* (Sept. 15, 2021), https://www.umnews.org/en/news/a-call-to-examine-united-methodist-real-estate (accessed Nov. 15, 2021). Also see Rick Reinhard, "Surplus Sacred Space: Reflections on the Impending Glut of US Church Property," *Journal of Urban Regeneration and Renewal* 14 (2021), pp. 247-254.

of mutual responsibility for one another.[12] As one community developer put it, "If we fail to adequately understand these changes—representing both challenges and opportunities—we may well lose vital community capacity that will not be easy or even possible to replicate."[13]

The innovation conversation in churches is wracked with problems, especially theological ones. We are lurching our way to the cross; we're a long way from getting this right. Still, something important happens when people see the gorilla: apart from the arrival of the Holy Spirit, I have no explanation for the electrifying missional vigor that explodes when people discover God at work on the slant. Helping ministry communities make the shift from forming blacksmiths to boilermakers to whatever ministry comes next is messy, disorienting work. But I cannot shake the sense that we are wrestling with an angel. As Christian social innovation provides new openings for ministry, we will be left with a limp, count on it. But the church must keep wrestling until the angel blesses us (Gen. 32:22-32).

I really wish we had a better word to describe this work. Innovation gets us part way there; but, like entrepreneurship (French for "undertaking in between," *entre* + *prendre*), the word innovation is so damaged by historical whiplash, so freighted with moral assumptions, and now so thoroughly aligned with start-up culture that it is hard to take back. Words like discipleship, witness, mission, transformation, change,

---

[12] See Robert D. Putnam, Bowling Alone: T*he Collapse and Revival of American Community* (New York: Simon & Schuster), 2000.

[13] Kendra Frye, project lead, "No Space for Community: The Value of Faith Buildings and the Effect of Their Loss in Ontario," *Faith and the Common Good* https://www.faithcommongood.org/community_spaces_faith_places_survey_results, July 16, 2020 (accessed November 15, 2021).

rebirth, even reformation also swim in these waters. But the word that seems to beg for our attention as we dust for God's fingerprints in this work is *vocation*.

For young people, the link between social innovation and vocation is especially vital. When youth and young adults think about making a difference in the world, they do not think about ministry; they think about Warby Parker and Tom's Shoes. Nor do most of them think about God. They are forging ahead on their own steam, which means they are pouring their all into *their* new thing, which is not necessarily God's "new thing."

This scenario begs for burnout. Even young people of faith often fail to connect their call as a member of the baptized with their desire to become a force for good in their communities. Here is a quote from an actual conversation I had with a young adult recently – a seminarian – who called me seeking vocational advice: "I love ministry," he told me. "But I'm thinking about nonprofit work, because I want to make a difference in the world, and you obviously can't do that through a church." To this young man, apparently, we feel love in church, but we actualize it elsewhere.

That needs to change.

The Miracle of Dunkirk

Because I work with social innovators, people often ask me: "What is the next 'big thing' you see on the horizon for ministry?" Presumably the task of academics is to scan the horizon, spot the next trend hurtling through space, and put everyone else on notice.

Here's the truth: I don't see a "next big thing" for ministry on the horizon. And I've looked.

What I see is Dunkirk – a flotilla of tiny boats slowly

coming into view: small experiments of a thousand shapes and sizes cresting on the horizon, all heading toward a shore where people are stuck, trapped in their hairballs, and see no way out. These little vessels of hope are the church, the ark of salvation, the holy vessel of God, in its countless forms. Some of these vessels are stout and seaworthy and have been at this for a long time. Others are new and untested. A lot of them don't look like they have many more trips across the channel left in them, and some barely look like boats at all. But they are all part of Christ's fleet, and they are all on the same mission. Frankly, for the people stuck on shore, it doesn't matter which boat they get on. What matters is that they *get on a boat,* a sanctuary God has sent to carry them home.

And until those boats arrive?

We will cling to our flotsam, and paddle toward shore.

APPENDICES
Ten Resources
for Getting Started

1. THE INNOVATION JOURNEY   45 minutes

"A ship is safe in harbor, but that's not what ships are for."

William Shedd (1820-1894), Presbyterian theologian[1]

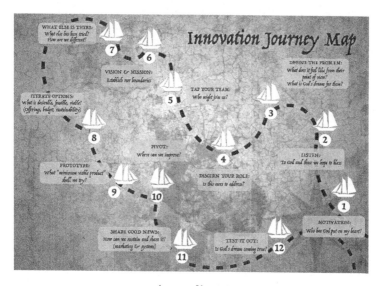

Appendix 1.1

---

[1]   John A. Shedd, *Salt from My Attic* (Portland, ME: Mosher Press, 1928).

What is the innovation journey?

Every innovation goes through a set of steps that transform an idea into action – that move your ministry idea from "concept to launch." This map identifies 12 "moments" in the Christian social innovator's journey.

Goal:

To locate your group or Expedition team on this map, and to create a timeline that includes each moment of the journey.

Materials:

This graphic and a calendar.

Objective:

Identify the ship on the map that best represents your group or Expedition team's progress so far and assign dates to the other ships based on your hoped-for launch date.

Discuss:

Have each person on your Expedition team or group locate the ship that best describes where you perceive your team to be on your innovation journey. Discuss. What is your hoped-for launch date for your new expedition or ministry project? Put it on a calendar. Make a timeline with arrival dates for the other parts of your innovation journey. (*The exercises here may help you.*)

2. HOW READY ARE YOU TO INNOVATE?   60 minutes

"Everyone thinks of changing the world; no one thinks of changing himself."

Leo Tolstoy[2]

What is an innovation readiness audit?

An innovation readiness audit is a brief but intentional look into a community's attitudes toward innovation and asks some honest questions about your community's culture in order to assess how ready you are to dive into an innovation process.

Goal:

To celebrate ways your congregation/ministry community has innovated in the past and to assess their readiness to start an innovation process.

Materials:

A panel consisting of the pastor or community leader, and two veterans from your congregation/ministry community, and an innovation readiness audit tool. Here are three (free) tools that you could choose from to start:

- Glean's *Innovation Readiness Self-Assessment*, part of their excellent "Spark Toolkit" for spiritual entrepreneurs, https://www.gleannetwork.org/spark-toolkit

- Strategyzer's *Innovation Readiness Tool* (written for secular organizations), Invincible_Company_Toolkit-innovation readiness.pdf

---

[2]   Leo Tolstoy, "Three Methods of Reform," *Pamphlets: Translated from the Russian* (Sydney, Australia: Wentworth Press, 2016).

- Viima's *Innovation Culture Toolkit* (written for secular organizations), https://www.viima.com/innovation-culture-toolkit

Objective:
To decide if your congregation or ministry community is saying *stop, caution,* or *go* in your innovation work.

Instructions:
- Host an "innovation audit panel" with your pastor/ministry leader and a couple longtime congregants (or veterans from your ministry community) as panelists.

- Share with them the definition of Christian social innovation that your group or Expedition team has chosen. Ask them questions like:

  ¤ In your memory, what's the most creative thing our congregation/ministry community has ever done? Was it in response to a need in our community? Talk about it.

  ¤ When you think of someone in our congregation/ministry community who always has (or had) a fresh way of looking at things – or some creative spark that just brought people joy – who do you think of? What is something they did that you remember?

  ¤ How is your congregation/ministry community innovating for love right now? How does that ministry add value to people's lives? How does it demonstrate Jesus' "upside down" way of seeing the world?

142

• Celebrate the ways your congregation/ministry community has innovated for love in the past, and the ways you may be doing so currently. *(For more buy-in, share these stories on your community's website, in a visible way in your gathering space, or in your email newsletter.)*

• Invite the panel to join you in taking an Innovation Readiness Self-Assessment (see *"Materials"* above). Discuss your answers. How do you think others in your ministry community would answer?

Discuss:
• Show your team an image of a stoplight. Do you think your congregation/ministry community is giving you a red, yellow, or green light on innovation? *(If you're unsure, invite a broader group to take your Innovation Readiness Self-Assessment and discuss their answers.)*

• Were there any responses that surprised you?

• Given the outcome of the inventory, what is your group or Expedition team's next step in innovating for love?

3. THE IMPORTANCE OF CONNECTION   30 minutes

"Chance favors the connected mind."

Stephen Johnson[3]

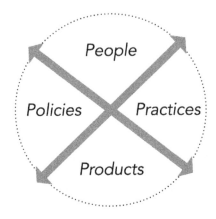

Appendix 3.1
Components Contributing to an Ecology of Innovation

What is an innovation ecosystem?

Here's a definition for our purposes: it is a collaborating set of people, practices, policies, and products whose synergy creates a hospitable environment for new ideas to take root and evolve.[4]

All definitions of innovation ecosystems share a basic premise: innovation emerges in cultures that promote *connections.* Media analyst Stephen Johnson argues

---

[3] See Stephen Johnson's illustrated talk, viewed more than five million times (https://www. youtube.com/watch?v=NugRZGDbPFU) based on his bestselling book, *Where Good Ideas Come From: The Natural History of Innovation* (New York: Riverhead Publishing, 2011).

[4] For one review of definitions, see Ove Granstrand and Marcus Holgersson, "Innovation Ecosystems: A Conceptual Review and a New Definition," *Technovation* 90-91 (February-March 2020) 102098, (https://doi.org/10.1016/j.technovation.2019.102098 (accessed July 4, 2021).

that the Enlightenment didn't become a hotbed of new philosophies until salons allowed people to share new ideas with one another. Silicon Valley wasn't Silicon Valley until coffee shops moved in, providing physical spaces for people with different skills and backgrounds, working on different kinds of projects, to meet and swap ideas. The more ways we have to connect (and with digital technology, the possibilities are endless) the more likely it is that my dormant, partial idea – what Johnson calls a "slow hunch" – will be awakened, reframed, and modified by yours, which opens new possibilities.[5]

In short, innovation requires a supportive ecology to emerge. Specifically, it requires a culture consisting of certain kinds of *people* (for example, those who are more open than closed, or more hopeful/trusting than suspicious/fearful), *practices* (collaboration, playfulness, action, etc.), *policies* (for instance, those that reward risk-taking and adaptability), and *products* (think: technology, gathering spaces, materials, etc.). Together, these factors create fertile soil for new possibilities.

Goal:
To become aware of multiple systems that must work together to create an innovative culture.

Materials
Stephen Johnson's 4-minute illustrated talk, *Where Good Ideas Come From,* https://www.youtube.com/watch?v=NugRZGDbPFU

---

[5] See Johnson. Idea generation can be just as effective online as in person. See Claire Cain Miller, "Do Chance Meetings at the Office Boost Innovation? There's No Evidence of It," *The New York Times* (June 23, 2001), https://www.nytimes.com/2021/06/23/upshot/remote-work-innovation-office.html (accessed July 6, 2021).

Objective:
To identify strengths and weaknesses in your congregation/ministry community's innovation ecosystem.

Instructions:
Explain what an innovation ecosystem is and watch the Stephen Johnson video.

Discuss:

- Has Johnson's thesis – that "chance favors the connected mind" – been true in your own experience?

- Has anyone in your group or Expedition team helped you turn a "slow hunch" into a ministry idea? Give examples.

- In your congregation/ministry community, where do "slow hunches" tend to collide? What changes (to space, schedule, people, practices, etc.) might increase opportunities for "slow hunch collisions"?

- Innovation ecosystems consist of *people, practices, policies*, and *products* that are hospitable to generating new ideas.

  ◻ Which of these subsystems are most supportive of innovation in your congregation/ministry community? (Give examples)

  ◻ Are any subsystems barriers to innovation in your community? (Give examples)

4. THE DESIGN PROCESS

50 minutes

"Your system is perfectly designed for the results you actually get."

Mark DeVries, pastor and entrepreneur

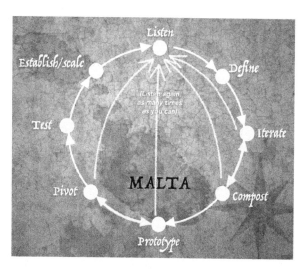

Appendix 4.1
"Moments" in an Innovation Process

What is an innovative design process?

Ask 10 people and you'll get 20 answers, but some common ones are described here.

Goal:

To introduce different components of an innovative design process.

Materials:

Markers, sticky notes

147

Objective:
Understand the basic rhythms of a design process and explore what it might look like for designing your ministry.

Instructions:
Read these FAQs about design processes and discuss the questions at the end.

1) What does an innovative design process look like?

Of course, it depends on who you ask – there are dozens to choose from, and none of them are exactly alike. But they do follow a basic pattern. Look at this list, and you will see that you've already been steeped in innovative design in some ways. Design's emphasis on listening and empathy feels especially familiar to people in ministry:

Listen	As you listen to the stories of people you want your new ministry to bless (end-users), notice what is said and unsaid as they share their struggles/joys around the problem you will tackle. Listen from their point of view. Empathize.
Define	Based on what you learn in the listening stage, define the problem you will address more specifically, from the end-user's point of view?
Iterate	Brainstorm ways to address the problem (include ideas from end-users if possible). Say "Yes, and…" to each idea, building on it. Pay attention to ideas that capture your imagination. Ask: "Why am I drawn to this idea? Is it desirable? Is it feasible? Is it viable? (If not, compost it.) Before moving on, ask: "Who else should we talk to? What motivation draws us to this idea?"
Compost	Since you can only implement one idea at a time, "compost" your other ideas – give back to God those ideas that you cannot implement at this time.

148

Prototype	See what you can learn by trying out your focal idea in a cheap, quick way
Pivot	Adjust your ministry idea to incorporate what you have learned from your prototypes: make changes, additions, or go back to the drawing board.
Test	Demonstrate your new improved idea by putting it in action
Scale	After you have been operating long enough that your new ministry is relatively secure, increase your capacity and expand and refine the ministry.

2) What is the design squiggle?

The *design squiggle* is a model that acknowledges the hot mess that starts every design process. This model views innovative design as an exercise that brings order out of chaos.

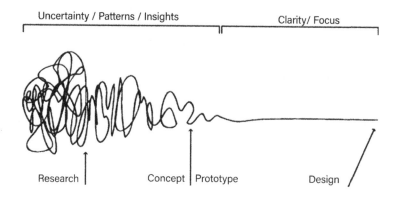

Appendix 4.2
The Design Squiggle (Damien Newman)[6]

---

[6] Terry Winograd, "Design Process Diagrams," Institute of Design at Stanford, https://hci. stanford.edu/dschool/resources/design-process/gallery.html (accessed June 26, 2021).

3) What is design thinking?

One popular design process is *design thinking*, championed by the design firm IDEO and the Hassno Plattner School of Design ("The D. School") at Stanford. Design thinking is a form of human-centered design – design that adds value to people's lives by creating products from the point of view (POV) of the user, not the designer.

Since its introduction in the 1970s, design thinking has become widely used to address social problems as well. It is commonly taught in schools from kindergarten through high school. Its distinctive feature is highlighting the role of empathy and time spent understanding the end-user. Design thinking focuses on five early stages in the innovation journey, often depicted in a "caterpillar" model:

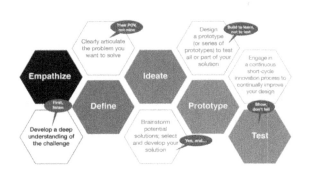

Appendix 4.3
5 Stages of Design Thinking[7]

---

[7]   Adapted from the Center for Innovation in Teaching and Learning, University of Illinois at Urbana-Champaign, https://citl.illinois.edu/paradigms/design-thinking (accessed June 26, 2021).

4) Isn't design just good old-fashioned problem-solving, only "prettier"?

That's a common misunderstanding. Design is not just how something looks – it's how it works, how it is situated in an ecology, what it does. That's why design is like problem-solving, though they have different emphases. For example:

- *Design processes explore the problem before focusing on a solution.* Traditional problem-solving is almost entirely focused on solutions, which carries the risk of becoming enamored with a "solution" prematurely, before we appreciate the problem. Once we mentally choose a solution, it's hard to let it go, even if it doesn't work well. That's why innovation experts advise: "Fall in love with your problem, not your solution."

- *Design processes aren't focused on one perfect solution.* Instead, innovators generate multiple solutions, try them out provisionally, adjust for what they learn along the way, and use playful experimentation and surprising juxtapositions to assess their usefulness.

- *Design processes don't require a clear answer before trying out a solution.* Innovators learn by doing; failure is a form of learning, so the sooner you fail, the faster you learn. Innovators do plenty of thinking before they act, of course, but they also have a "bias toward action," which means: "If in doubt, do."

- *Design processes are most useful for complex problems with uncertain solutions.* Processes of innovation are best for addressing "wicked" problems that have no clear answers, in which solutions can emerge after some trial and error (e.g., developing a COVID-19 vaccine), but clear-cut problem-solving is better for situations that are straightforward and/or need immediate intervention (e.g., helping a choking victim).

- *Design processes offer provisional, not permanent, solutions.* Innovation and design are ongoing processes of trial-and-error; innovators "build to learn" rather than "build to last." If a solution doesn't work, it is discarded or changed to try again.

Discuss:

- Write each stage of the design process in Figure A-1 on a sticky note (one stage per sticky note). Pass them out to your Expedition team or group members and let them arrange them in the order that makes sense to them. Compare their list to Figure A-1.

- Discuss any steps that aren't clear.

- Introduce the *design squiggle* and *design thinking*. Ask team members if they have seen these before, and if so, to describe their experience with them.

- Discuss the pros and cons of an innovative design process vs. problem-solving. What are the differences? When are each most useful?

- *Ask:* Has our congregation/organization ever "fallen in love with a solution" so much that we couldn't let it go – even after it stopped working? Share stories. In these cases, what might have helped us let go sooner?

More resources:

For an excellent group introduction to design thinking, play *Mission Possible* (available in online and physical versions) with your group or Expedition team – the more teams that play, the better it is. Available at www. rootedgood.org (prices online).

5. THE EMPATHY CONVERSATION   60-120 minutes

"It is much easier to design for someone you love."

Maggie Zhang, IDEO, Palo Alto, California

Why Empathy Conversations Matter

Chennai, India

Jane Chen, Linus Liang, Naganund Murty, and Rahul Panicker met as students at Stanford University, in a multidisciplinary course called "Design for Extreme Affordability." Their class assignment was straightforward: design an infant incubator that would cost 1% of the cost ($20,000) of a traditional incubator.

Since 40% of premies are born in India, the team decided to spend spring break at a hospital there, talking to doctors. When they arrived, a doctor led them to the hospital's NICU, where all four incubators sat empty. "Where are the babies?" one student asked. "Sadly," the doctor said, "they die before they get here. Most are born in the villages, four or five hours away. Mothers can't keep their babies warm enough to survive the trip."

Since premature babies lack body fat, they can't regulate their body temperatures, making hypothermia fatal. Listening to the doctor made the students realize that they didn't need to redesign a hospital incubator; they had to figure out how to keep babies warm in remote rural villages. That meant they needed to talk to people who most needed a solution: mothers of premature infants in rural villages.

So, the students made a crucial decision: forget about the class (and their grade) and take a bus to villages to talk to mothers. Those conversations revealed many things the students had not considered: the solution must work without electricity (villages had none), it had to be cheap (mothers were very poor), and – a surprising discovery – it needed to be transparent (students noticed mothers kept checking their babies' chests to see if they were still breathing). The device had to be reassuring as well as effective.

What the students designed was an incubator that looked nothing like an incubator: it was a tiny sleeping bag, warmed by a reusable pouch of melted wax that could be re-melted by placing it in boiling water (no electricity required). A plastic window in the front of the swaddling bag let mothers monitor their baby's breathing. The whole thing cost less than $25.

Since 2011, *Embrace Innovations* has saved the lives of more than 200,000 infants in 20 countries…all because students listened to those most affected: mothers in rural villages.

What is an empathy conversation?
Empathy conversations are chats between users
and designers, used in human-centered design to
create products from the user's perspective. These
conversations help us better understand a problem
from the point of view of those experiencing a specific
problem (*see inset above*).

An empathy conversation is a cross between an interview
and a chat. Your goal is to understand feelings and
behaviors, not collect "answers" – though people's
answers are often the way to get to these feelings and
behaviors. Ideally, empathy conversations are done in
pairs, so one interviewer asks questions, and one takes
notes and observes what isn't talked about (context,
nonverbal behavior, etc.)

Goal:
To understand the perspective of the people you hope
your ministry will bless, and to design a ministry that
genuinely scratches where they itch.

Materials:
Time and a list of questions.

Objective:
Conduct 3-5 empathy conversations with people
experiencing the problem you hope to address.

Instructions:
• Set a deadline for when empathy conversations will
  be completed. (We suggest a week or two, no longer.
  The more conversations people have, the better
  their solutions will be – but energy will be better if

conversations are fairly close together.) <u>Note</u>: *If you anticipate scale or wide impact, schedule as many interviews as it takes before they all start sounding alike.*

- Read "What Is an Empathy Conversation?" above.

- Identify **3-5 adults** affected by the problem you wish to address – people who have been "entangled in grave clothes," to use the Scriptural metaphor. Follow the instructions below for conducting an Empathy Conversation. (<u>Note</u>: *If talking to minors, remember to* always *secure parental permission first, and have a second adult present during the conversation, which should be conducted in a public space.*)

- With your group or Expedition team, agree on **3-5 questions** *(see chart, below)* to help the conversation get started.

Discuss:
- Ask your group or Expedition team how your congregation/organization listens to people that you hope a new ministry will bless. How well do we do that?

- Bring back notes from your conversations to your Expedition team or group meeting, and discuss what you observed.

- What kind of new ministry might unbind the people in your neighborhood?

Conducting an Empathy Conversation

Rule of thumb:	Pro tips:
Meet face-to-face	• Do one conversation at a time • In a pinch, zoom will do • Listen in pairs: one to guide the conversation, and one to take notes, observe body language, emotional tone, context, etc. • Plan 40-50 minutes per conversation
Use neutral questions	• Make a short question list to prompt interviewees to share stories about their experience with the problem • Avoid leading questions • Questions should explore, reflect, probe, analyze, clarify, reveal feelings – not just "get an answer" YES: What do you think about the nursery at church? NO: What frustrates you about the nursery at church? YES: Tell me about the last time you... NO: Tell me about your problem with...
Encourage stories	• Avoid anything that can be answered in one word. • Stories say more about our motivations, mindsets, and behaviors than answers do. YES: Tell me about the last time you took communion. NO: Have you ever taken communion? YES: What happened the last time you were on the food truck? NO: Is the food truck important to you?
Ask why	• Be a learner...be curious. • Don't assume you know the answer • Ask "why?" (people often don't volunteer a "why" without being asked)
Chase rabbits	• If something brings up a lot of energy in the conversation, follow it (tangents may reveal more about our true concerns than planned Q&A)
Observe nonverbals	• Actions speak louder than words (what our bodies convey is often more truthful than what we verbalize)
Silence is okay	• Don't be the one who breaks the silence; let your interviewee bring up the next thought.
Remember that "being heard" is rare and sacred	• Receive people's stories with awe and wonder: you are on holy ground

6. THE WAGON WHEEL   30-40 minutes

(Used with permission from Ministry Incubators,
www.ministryincubators.com)

*"The risk of a wrong decision is preferable to the
terror of indecision."*

Maimonides (1135-1204 C.E.)[8]

The Brain Kitchen
Marion, Indiana

Amanda Drury had no intention of participating in The Wagon
Wheel exercise; she was attending a Ministry Incubators
training event as an observer, to get some ideas for a class she
taught at Indiana Wesleyan University. When the time came for
the exercise, however, there was an odd number of people – so
Amanda stepped in as an extra partner.

The first question required her to think of a problem in her
community she cared about. She had 30 seconds to think of one.
The second question asked for an idea that would address that
problem. Again, she had 30 seconds to think of one.

By the end of the exercise, *The Brain Kitchen* was born – a
trauma-informed after-school program that creates "wonder and
resilience" for low-income children in Marion, Indiana. Amanda
made some phone calls on breaks during the event, and had her
first funding and space leads before she got home.

The Brain Kitchen partners college students trained in trauma-
related care and child development with elementary-aged
children, and includes a range of activities for enrichment and
fun (field trips, visits from therapy dogs, and concerts with
local musicians are common). But the key activity is cooking. In
designing *The Brain Kitchen* (the zombie reference is intentional,
to make the program more appealing to boys), Amanda also
wanted to address the food insecurity that haunts these children
and their families. For many children, school lunches are their

---

[8] Cited by Jose Suarez, "The Risk of a Wrong Decision Is Preferable to the Terror of Indecision,"
LinkedIn (August 9, 2019), https://www.linkedin.com/pulse/risk-wrong-decision-prefera-
ble-terror-indecision-jos%C3%A9-su%C3%A1rez-c%C3%B3rdova/ (accessed July 7, 2021).

only full meal of the day. On weekends, food is scarce. So, The *Brain Kitchen* invites children to "make bread, bake bread, and break bread." On Fridays, each child takes home a meal that they themselves have prepared for their families, along with two loaves of bread – one to keep, and one to give away.

The Brain Kitchen received the Duke Leadership's "Traditioned Innovation" Award, has been featured in local and national news, and briefly added a pop-up tea shop as well, to expand its networks and income streams. But at the end of the day, it's about the bread of life – communion in the most real sense.

Objective:

To test-drive the basic features of a MAP (ministry action plan) that addresses a problem you care about. *(To download the wagon wheel exercise, go to www. ministryincubators.com)*

Materials:

A stopwatch or watch with a second hand, a whistle or chime that makes a loud noise, and a large colorful flag to wave (big enough to get people's attention when they're doing something else).

Notes for the leader:

• This exercise uses "timeboxing" to create short windows for thinking, which increases creative output. You can shorten the time for some questions to keep the energy high, but we do *not* recommend lengthening the time for any answers. The short timeframes are designed to keep the tension high, which improves the energy of the experience.

• Don't forget to give the extra instruction after Round 3*

• The story in the inset (above) about *The Brain Kitchen* may be shared to encourage participants who think this exercise is...nuts.

- Don't skip the debrief! This is where the discovery happens, and it's usually gold!

Instructions:

- Divide the group in half. Ask the first half to form a circle, standing about 2-3 feet apart, facing inward.

- Ask the second group to enter the circle, find a partner, and face them (like you're going to shake hands). You now have two circles, an inner and outer circle, facing each other.

- Say to the group:

  ¤ This exercise is like "speed dating" a business plan for a new expedition or ministry idea. If you don't have a ministry idea yet – don't worry, you will soon.

  ¤ We will have 10 rounds of about 90 seconds each.

    - For each round, I will give you a question to answer.

    - Both partners have to answer – so that's about 45 seconds each.

    - The outside person will go first.

    - When I wave this flag like this (demonstrate), it means it's time for the other person in your pair to answer the question.

  ¤ Each time you hear the chime (or whistle), you will switch partners this way: the outside circle will stand still, and the inside circle will move one partner to your left. Let's practice that:

    - Leader: Ring the chime.

    - Participants: Switch partners as described.

    - Leader: Compliment them on the chaos!

▢ So let's do a practice round. Ready?

- Leader: Who in your neighborhood does your heart break for, and why?

- Participants: Answer the question, as directed.

- Leader: Wave the flag after 30 seconds. Ring the chime after 60 seconds.

WAGON WHEEL QUESTIONS

1.	What idea has God given you, and who will it help?	60-90 seconds
2.	Why do you care so much about this idea?	60-90 seconds
3.*	What is the name of your idea for ministry? What are you going to call it? (*Extra instruction after Round 3: From now on, be sure to start by sharing the name of your ministry idea, so your new partner knows what you're talking about!)	60-90 seconds
4.	Why should Christians do this, and not just leave it to general good will?	60-90 seconds
5.	Where is Jesus hiding in your idea? Is there a Scripture passage driving your thinking?	60-90 seconds
6.	What core programs/activities will you offer?	60-90 seconds
7.	How will you make money? How will it be sustainable?	60-90 seconds
8.	What is the fleece you're laying out? (Judges 6:39-40) How are you saying to God, "Lord, I'll do this IF..." (fill in the blank)	60-90 seconds
9.	It's 10 years from now, and your idea has succeeded beyond your wildest dreams. What does it look like?	60-90 seconds
10.	What's your next step? Not next year – next week!	60-90 seconds

After doing the exercise, discuss:

Was there any idea in the group that really inspired you? Or maybe someone whose idea helped you find a missing piece of your own idea?

How did *your idea* change as you went through this process?

How did *you* change as you went through this process?

7. CHASING GOD'S DREAM[9]   30 minutes

> *"A vision is not just a picture of what could be; it is an appeal to our better selves, a call to become something more."*
>
> **Rosabeth Moss Kanter**

Note: The Changemaker Church Movement's R.I.S.K. curriculum, created by Karen Kehlet and Kim Jones of Los Altos United Methodist Church (see inset, p.66) taught me this simple way of connecting our ideas with God's vision. The "dream statement" has two advantages for Christian social innovators:

- It immediately places our idea in the service of God's dream.

- It reminds us that we do this because of "who" (and "Who") this work is for.

The R.I.S.K. approach caused me to change the way I teach theological vision-casting. This (adapted) version is inspired by an exercise used in their beta phase.

What is a dream statement?

A *dream statement*, or theological vision statement, describes the *part* of God's dream you want to help come true in the next 3-5 years.

Goal:

To declare the part of God's dream for a particular group, or part of creation, that you want to help materialize.

Materials:

Dream statement mad lib, pens, newsprint.

---

9   Used with permission from The Changemaker Church Movement, https://thechangemak-erinitiative.org/news/2020/10/14/announcing-the-changemaker-church-project

Objective: To state how your project emerges from a vision of the Reign of God.

Instructions:

In some settings, we talk about the problems our ideas will help solve. But as Christians, we don't start with problems – we start with God's vision for creation, the Reign of God, a world without suffering. You can't do everything with one project, so pick the one part of God's dream for a specific group of people or part of creation that your project will help make come true. (We think you should write it out.)

YOUR DREAM STATEMENT

"We will chase God's dream for _____

[a specific group of people or part of creation]

so that _____."

[what it looks like when God's dream comes true for them]

Appendix 7.1

Examples:

- "We will chase God's dream for *ostracized sex workers in Buffalo* so that *they will feel safe, known, and prayed for.*"

- "We will chase God's dream for *hungry elementary schoolchildren in Marion* so that *they will have a safe place after school and food on the weekends.*"

- "We will chase God's dream for *teenaged musicians who are on the margins of churches* so that *they can use their talent for worship.*"

163

Discuss:

• Invite everyone in your group or Expedition team to share his/her dream statement.

• *Ask*: What story or passage from Scripture comes to mind when you think about your dream statement?

  ◘ Write the key verse on your newsprint.

  ◘ Circle the words that speak most loudly to you in that passage.

  ◘ Ask: How does your ministry reflect the circled words?

  Example:

  ◘ 2 Cor. 9:8, "God is able to provide you with every blessing in abundance, so that by always having enough of everything, you may share abundantly in every good work"

• *If you have time:* Work as a team to create a "Side-of-the-Bus Motto" for your project that captures the words you circled in the Bible passage. The idea is to come up with a "short, sweet and swallowable" phrase that is explicitly inspired by your Scriptural passage, in a way that is easy for people to grasp quickly (i.e., as a bus drives by). Write your motto on the newsprint with your Scriptural passage. At the end, each group can share their Scripture passage and their motto.

Examples:

- 2 Cor. 9:8, "God is able to provide you with every ***blessing in abundance***, so that by always having ***enough*** of everything, you may ***share*** abundantly in every good work" (for an after-school program for food insecure children)
  Your motto might be: "Abundance to share"

- Psalm 34:8, "***Taste*** and ***see*** that the Lord is ***good***" (for a muffin-baking ministry that sold muffins to college students on their way to morning classes at bus stops)
  Your motto might be: "Taste and see"

- Philippians 4:13, "I can do ***all things*** through the ***Lord*** who ***strengthens*** me" (for a church-based weight-training program)
  Your motto might be:"By God, You're Strong!" (Runner up: "Holy Biceps, Batman!")

8. MISSION MAD LIBS   25-30 minutes

"As the Father has sent me, so I send you."

Jesus, John 20:21

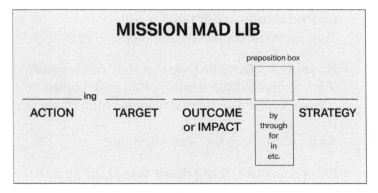

Figure 8.1
The 8-word Mission Statement

What is a mission statement?

A *mission statement* describes what your ministry
does, for whom, and at what level. Mission means
"sent": your mission statement declares what you
think God has sent you to do. If you are reading this
book as part of The Great Expedition, you are using
The Great Commission as your mission statement.
Your Christian social innovation, then, is in the
service of The Great Commission. The mission
statement for your Christian social innovation spells
out how it contributes to this larger goal.

Some people think mission statements should be
8-words or less, so everyone in the organization can
repeat it at the drop of a hat. Other people like to have a
longer mission statement (for internal use) and a shorter

one (a "mantra") for marketing purposes. Even if you expand your mission statement later, it's good discipline to keep the core idea simple. In the words of Guy Kawasaki, make it short, sweet, and swallowable.

Goal:
To clarify the nature of your expedition or ministry plan before building out its details.

Materials:
Paper, pens, large newsprint, masking tape or giant sticky note (1 per team).

Notes to the leader:

- Do this exercise *after* each group or Expedition team has:

  ◻ Settled on an idea they want to try.

  ◻ Clarified who their ministry is for – *who* do you want this ministry to bless?

  ◻ Had a discussion about *why* you are doing this ministry as an act of faith (the theological vision).

- It's not a crime to use more than 8 words, but you'll be surprised how much using the 8-word format will clarify your ministry plan.

Objective:
Write an 8-word (or less) mission statement for your ministry plan.

Instructions:
- Divide the group into teams. Each group can work on its own ministry idea, or each team can provide different versions of a mission statement for the same project. Review the definitions at the top of this page.

- Copy *Appendix 8.1* on a flip chart , whiteboard, or slide
- Explain the word categories in *Aplpendix 8.1*:

Category	Pro tip	Example: "We are..."
Action (verb)	Helps if it ends in "-ing"	...saving whales from extinction by eliminating ocean plastic.
Target audience (noun)	Who your ministry benefits (be specific)	...improving local teen health with church community gardens
Outcome (result-a)	What will happen if you succeed	...helping high school girls tell their stories through dance.
Impact (result-b)	The measurable difference you will make	...using mentors to help youth become FAA-certified drone pilots
Strategy (preposition)	The vehicle you will use to make change happen	...preventing LGBTQ youth suicide through harbor families

- Take 10 minutes as a team to fill in your mad lib.
  - ¤ *Pro tips:*
    - Choose either an outcome or an impact (sometimes they are the same).
    - You can rearrange the categories.
- Teams: Read your mad lib to the whole group.
  - ¤ *Pro tip*:
    - Post your mad lib on newsprint or a giant sticky note.
    - Add your team's description of who your ministry benefits, your theological vision, and core values to the same large sheet of paper.
- *Optional:* After everyone has shared, go back to your team and make any additions/corrections you want to make.

9. HOW-NOW-WOW [10]　　　　　　　　50 minutes

"I always imagined when I was a kid that adults had some kind of inner toolbox full of shiny tools: the saw of discernment, the hammer of wisdom, the sandpaper of patience. But then when I grew up I found that life handed you these rusty bent old tools – friendships, prayer, conscience, honesty – and said "do the best you can with these, they will have to do." And mostly, against all odds, they do."

Anne Lamott [11]

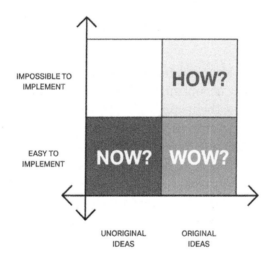

Appendix 9.1
How-Now-Wow Matrix [12]

---

[10]　This exercise is commonly used in design thinking and idea-evaluation workshops, and its origins are unclear, but it seems to have been adapted from a Dutch resource, *Creativity Today* (Amsterdam: BIS Publishers, 2009) by Igor Byttebier and Ramon Vullings. The book is available in English online at https://issuu.com/bls_publishers/docs/creativity_today (accessed August 21, 2021).

[11]　Anne Lamott, *Traveling Mercies: Some Thoughts on Faith* (New York: Anchor Books, 2000), 103.

[12]　Image taken from The Red-Yellow School's interpretation of the how-now-wow matrix, https://www.youtube.com/watch?v=Wwz1ucHafqA (accessed August 21, 2021).

What makes a good idea?

Every new ministry starts with a bank of ideas – some of them fanciful, some of them feasible, some of them remarkable but difficult, some of them ordinary but easy.

Just because an idea is new and original doesn't make it a good investment of time, energy, prayer, and hope. The trifecta for success for any innovation is *desirability* (do people want it?), *feasibility* (can we do it?) and *viability* (will it work?). If any one of these variables is missing, the project sinks.

Here's how to read the How-Now-Wow grid:

How:

Our moonshot ideas are *How?* ideas. These offerings would certainly be amazing, but we don't have what we need to make them happen at this time. Ideas are presently beyond our reach. That doesn't mean God won't open a door later, but for now our *How?* ideas operate as goals, not actual offerings. By definition, moonshots seem impossible – apart from God. But since God just might bring the proper set of variables together one day to make them happen, the best response to a moonshot offering is not "no," but "not yet."

Now:

Your *Now* quadrant is made up of "low hanging fruit" ideas – easy to offer, though not very original. *Now* activities may or may not be a good use of your time. If they distract you from your core mission, ignore them. Since lots of other organizations offer something similar, no one is harmed if you take a pass. Sometimes, however, *Now* activities and products are needed urgently, are on-mission and do not distract from your core offering. In those cases, they can introduce people to your ministry. Ben and Jerry's, for example, is known for its exotic ice cream flavors (Phish Food, Chunky Monkey, Cherry Garcia), all designed to provide a "euphoric customer experience."[13] But the first flavor Ben and Jerry's offered? Vanilla.

Wow:

This is your sweet spot, and where you want to invest most of your time and resources. They are desirable but difficult – but they are worth the investment. *Wow* offerings and activities are your ministry's signature; people will know you because of them. They are what make your ministry special. God has given you what you need to make them happen, even if you must stretch a little to get there.

	HOW	NOW	WOW
Description	Missional moonshots	Low-hanging fruit	The perfect activity for your mission
Reaction	"Great idea! But how? We don't currently have what it takes to offer this."	"That's so obvious, we can do that tomorrow!"	"This is 100% on point for us! We cannot be who we are without offering this to people!"
Bottom line	These activities or products are impossible to offer until God opens a door to make it happen	These activities or products won't set you apart in any meaningful way, and they might distract from your core offerings; but if they help others, are on-mission, and don't distract, you have little to lose by offering them	The activities and products your ministry is known for. They are desirable and difficult, but they are core to your mission, and you are uniquely called and equipped to deliver them.

Appendix 9.2
Reading the How-Now-Wow Matrix

[13] Alliston Ackerman and Alarice Padilla, "Ben & Jerry's: Quality from Cow to Cone," *Consumer Goods Technology* (October 9, 2013), https://consumergoods.com/ben-jerrys-quality-cow-cone (accessed August 21, 2021).

Goal:

After you have brainstormed the kinds of activities your ministry will offer; this exercise will help you evaluate and prioritize those ideas.

Materials:

A brainstorm list of ideas for your ministry; newsprint, butcher paper or a whiteboard; and sticky notes.

Objective:

To discern which ideas have core strength and seem to match the capacities God has given you to work with – and which ideas probably won't work.

Instructions:

- Draw a How-Now-Wow grid on newsprint and put each idea from your "What Will We Offer?" brainstorm on a separate sticky note.

- Locate each sticky note in one of the quadrants. (Some people call the empty quadrant "Ciao" – for ideas you are definitely ruling out.)

- Decide if you have any additional constraints that should be considered as you eliminate ideas (e.g., does a ministry have to launch by a certain date? does an idea have to satisfy a certain leader? etc.) If so, adjust the quadrants accordingly.

- Once you have placed each idea in a quadrant, eliminate all ideas except three per quadrant.

- Discuss with your team the virtues of the ideas you have left (we like the questions in Figure 9.3 as a way to vet these ideas). Eliminate one more sticky note in each quadrant.

- Decide which of the remaining activities/products you will offer first and second.

How to evaluate your ideas:

Of course, your team will immediately begin assessing ideas as soon as they are on the grid – but we love the questions Brian Jones of Innove Studios (https://innovestudios.org) uses to help Christian social innovators choose their ideas well (*see Figure 9.3*):

Is it fun?	• Does it motivate passion, joy, and enthusiasm to serve others? • Can you reasonably get others on board? • Does it make us want to innovate for Jesus?
Is it feasible?	• Does it have a reasonable shot at succeeding? • Do we know what to measure for success? • Do we have the skills, resources, and calling to pull it off? • Do we understand the community well enough to know it will work? • Do we have the right team for the job?
Is it a fit?	• Does it fit our mission as a church? • Does it represent Jesus? • Are we motivated by something besides profit? • Do our outcomes exhibit the fruits of the Spirit? • Does our idea inspire others to share in God's work?

Figure 9.3
How to Vet an Idea[14]

Additional resources:

Once you have selected your initial offerings and created a ministry action plan for how it should operate, give it a "stress test." Ask each member of

---

[14] Brian Jones, "Student Innove," unpublished curriculum, Serial No. 867-EDG-309 (November 20. 2017).

your group or Expedition team to think of a scenario that would place pressure on your ministry (e.g., a global pandemic where everyone stays home, a 30% drop in funding, loss of a key pastoral leader, etc.). Discuss out how well you think your ministry would weather each of these stressors and strengthen your ministry action plan accordingly.

Alternatively:

Play the card game *"Blow Up Your Idea"* with your group or Expedition team (available for sale at www. ministryincubators.com).

10. THE FEED TRUCK: A CASE STUDY
ABOUT A PENGUIN   30-45 minutes

"A penguin is something that ought to fly but somehow just doesn't...We're like the penguins. We can't fly, but maybe we can learn to swim".

Ginny & Georgia, "Feelings are Hard," February 24, 2021 [15]

The Feed Truck, originally a campus ministry outreach of my congregation, was the first food truck in our county. Demand was great – too great. That is part of the reason, after seven years, it is no longer operating, although the stated (true) reason is that the engine

is shot and, at 300,000+ miles, is beyond repair. In the truck's last year of operation, it broke down on its way to more gigs than it got to.

But there's more to the story.

The Feed Truck – a retro-fitted bread truck with an eye-popping white and yellow "new rustic" design – was designed to take ministry to college students in the form of "hand-crafted egg sandwiches" with signature house-made jams (and they were out of this world). We also made meals for local homeless shelters and, on occasion, served food to others in need. What mattered to us was not just what The Feed Truck did; it mattered how we did it – paying fair wages to our occasional employees,

---

[15] Ginny & Georgia, "Feelings Are Hard" Netflix (Episode 9, Season 1, February 24, 2021).

tithing our profits to local food justice organizations, creating a work atmosphere of care and joy on the truck itself. The core mission was motivated by the 58,000 college students who study in our county, and the fact that our little church, which was mostly young adults, was near none of them. At the time, mainline Protestant campus ministries in our area were either non-existent or tragically dysfunctional. In any case, we decided the solution – if students couldn't come to us – was to bring *The Feed Truck* to them.

Two things you should know before reading further. First: you can blame me in part for this ministry, since I helped get *The Feed Truck* started. I did, and do, believe in its potential for ministry. Second: take "little church" literally: our flock consists of 30 to 40 people on a mission (known by all) to "Feed More Sheep." More on that in a minute.

Christian Social Entrepreneurship: What Could Go Wrong?

As a concept, *The Feed Truck* was brilliant. It was the brainchild of a seminarian who later became our church's part-time pastor as well, and the idea quickly caught the imagination of the whole church. Before seminary our pastor had been in management with Starbucks, and opening new stores was her specialty. Starting a food truck ministry seemed like a natural fit. *The Feed Truck*, with its "Keep Your Sunny Side Up" motto and farm-fresh sheep graphics, was quickly a fixture around town. It was an event on wheels, and everyone wanted in. Volunteers in bright yellow T-shirts stood around the truck to converse with students standing in line, waiting on their cold brew. (We flirted with spinning off a summer ministry that served cold brew on campus from a three-wheeler, called *The Feed Trike*.)

For six years *The Feed Truck* was our congregation's primary form of outreach, but sustainability eluded us. Every year we pivoted to a different financial arrangement, even adding a pop-up café in a congregation across the street from campus. On the surface, both the truck and the pop-up café were smash hits; our denomination sent film crews and seminarians got field ed credit for making bacon and breakfast burritos. But when the truck's engine blew (after two seasons patching it together), we had to face facts. We had done a lot of things right, mainly by offering a quality product and an experience of "church" that people weren't embarrassed to claim. And it was a lot of fun. But it was also a lot of work, and we made (at least) four mistakes common among churches experimenting with social innovation, that taught us more lessons than we can count:

Lesson #1: Lose the charity mindset.

All ministries require capital: spiritual, human, intellectual, material, and of course financial. Many congregations view money as a "necessary evil" for ministry; the less said about it, the better. But money is not the "bad guy" to ministry's "good guy" in Christian social innovation. As we have pointed out, every congregation has a business model – and if it doesn't work, the church folds.

At the end of the day, even though The Feed Truck was its own LLC, we ran it more like a charity than a social enterprise, funding it mostly with donations and grants rather than capitalizing on a food truck's inherent capacity to generate income. Part of it was our naivete to "best practices" of social enterprise: we never established a rainy-day fund, diversified our revenue streams, looked for ways to monetize the truck's "brand" in the off-season, or booked enough "gigs" to do more than break even. (Eventually we moved to a cheaper all-volunteer workforce; this meant fewer events and happier volunteers, but it solidified our self-image as a charity rather than a social enterprise.) The "money part" was largely left to our pastor, who did what pastors trained to do: she sought donations. *The Feed Truck*'s lifespan became linked to the cultivation and longevity of donors.

All in all, our congregation had difficulty imagining *The Feed Truck*'s economic model as a social enterprise. Volunteers came out of the woodwork when *The Feed Truck* gave food away for free; but they dried up when it came time for-profit events, like selling at the local farmers' market, which generated cash to make "free food events" possible. When money ran short, we did the "Christian thing" and dipped into reserves to make salaries whole, floating employees without clarifying expected deliverables in return. Hiring regular staff might have solved this – but that would have required more for-profit activities to pay them. At the end of the day, we did charity work, not social enterprise.

Congregations are deeply entrenched in the charity mindset, despite the fact that charity – absolutely essential in times of crisis – has been widely critiqued as an ongoing way to relieve suffering.[16] As an ongoing practice, charity seldom transforms communities; it

<hr>

[16] See Robert Lupton, *Toxic Charity: How the Church Hurts Those They Help and How to Reverse It* (San Francisco: HarperOne), 2011.

often creates unhealthy dependencies instead. Very often it becomes a form of "mutual using" in which helpers and those helped enter into an unspoken pact: "We donate these goods and services to you, and in return you let us feel good about ourselves." Our theology is at stake here, not our pocketbooks.

Lesson #2: God does not need all ministry to happen through churches.

It never occurred to us that we might have our leadership model for *The Feed Truck* backward. Because our pastor was instrumental in launching the vision for this ministry – and because she happened to have a business background – we thought she was the natural leader for *The Feed Truck* ministry, and we thought our congregation was its natural host. We assumed that having a food truck ministry meant that it needed to belong, in practice if not deed, to the church.

We were wrong. We made the common mistake of assuming the pastor is the primary innovator, and our job is to support her in doing it. But despite the fact that some pastors are natural innovators, pastors *need* not be the chief innovators. Instead, the pastor's job is to inspire *others* to heed God's call to create for the common good, to equip people with theological frameworks for this work, and to bless every disciple's creative efforts to heal the world. God needs churches to explore new approaches to ministry, and God needs pastors to lead them in doing so...which is different from charging pastors with creating new ministries and then expecting the pastor to make them work.

There is an obvious alternative, which we completely overlooked: instead of expecting the pastor to be a food truck operator on the side, we could have looked for someone called to be a *food truck operator* who want to live out her faith through her work. What might happen if a wildly enthusiastic faith community made supporting a local Christian entrepreneur part of its mission? While our pastor was still a seminarian, she was this kind of an entrepreneur: she gave heart and soul to creating a food truck ministry. It was her "baby." She went to bed thinking about how to serve God through a food truck, she woke up in the morning thinking about how to make it work. Through all of this, our congregation walked beside her, supporting her, and championing her gifts. Once she became the church's pastor, however, the roles shifted. We were no longer helping her launch her ministry through *The Feed Truck;* she was suddenly helping us launch ours.

This was an inadvertent but fatal turn for our relationship with *The Feed Truck*. What our congregation (mostly 20-somethings) does best is cheer, support, and provide a spiritual community for young adults launching new plans. Yet instead of midwifing a new ministry and releasing it into the world, we became its owners, concerned with survival. The point, after all, was not to own a food truck; the point was to make a food truck ministry available to the students and community we hoped to serve – which made the matter of ownership irrelevant. What if we sought out a food truck operator who saw her work as an act of faith, walked alongside her, wrapped her in a loving and supportive community, and helped her obtain a truck? Then we could have poured ourselves out helping her business (ministry) flourish, helping her frame her work as a vocation, and blessing her ministry as an extension of ours.

Social innovators abound who need support and community, and some entrepreneurs do indeed approach their work as a calling. There's nothing wrong with churches operating ministries as innovative businesses, of course, but it is equally powerful – and perhaps a better use of human capital – for congregations to support others in their callings to own coffeeshops, teach music, care for children, build health clinics, or create art rather than make churchy versions of these and hope these people will help. It is not necessary that these people replace the business sector to transform it. The existing business sector includes people yearning for God's transformation – and in these cases, a faith community's support could make a life-giving difference.

Lesson #3: Good intentions are not good ministry.
The Feed Truck revealed how often our good intentions obscured good ministry. Most notably, we needed to come clean about who this ministry really helped. Congregational "outreach" or mission work commonly focuses on transactional relationships. In other words, we tell ourselves that we exist to serve those who avail themselves of our ministry – in our case, the students buying sandwiches from the truck – when in fact we are the real beneficiaries.

It's a common delusion. We intended *The Feed Truck* to bless those who purchased egg sandwiches and coffee from the truck. Especially because we had to fill out reports for various funders that quantified our impact, it was easy to confuse "counting customers" with impact. Inadvertently, we began to think of the truck's ministry as ministry *to* rather than ministry *with*. But people who came to the truck's window weren't looking for a church; they were looking for an egg sandwich.

The people working on the truck, however, were another story. For them, this ministry was life-giving. Early employees got their first taste of theology and people of faith through their work with the truck; volunteers found being behind the counter a real source of joy. Al, who at age 78 was the truck's most tireless yellow-shirted "greeter," loved talking to people waiting in line for their coffee. Spontaneous singing would break out by the cash register; questions about faith were posed by the grill. It might have been hard to assess our impact on our customer base but being part of the truck's crew visibly grew disciples by deepening friendships, opening holy conversations, and creating sacred spaces for confession, discernment, and joy.

Lesson #4: Every ministry needs a champion – who is not the pastor. No one will ever accuse our small congregation of lack of vision, but we could easily be guilty of overestimating our capacity. (Pro tip: We should have tested our bandwidth on a minimum viable product, like *The Feed Trike*, before going all in on *The Feed Truck*. Next time.) We created a fatal cocktail of overestimating our energy and over-relying on our pastor for day-to-day operations. Little wonder that, by the time the engine quit, the pastor, board, and many volunteers were ready to quit as well.

Making *The Feed Truck* a full-time ministry might have strengthened its financial profile by devoting more time to sales, fundraising and donor relationships, but the bigger factor in the success of any ministry – full-time or not – is that it has a champion, someone whose primary reason for getting up in the morning to is to serve God through this ministry. However, *The Feed Truck's* viability lay disproportionately in the hands of the pastor – whose reason for getting up in the morning was to serve God through a different ministry (our congregation). The split-focus underscored what seasoned pastors know and rookie pastors forget: you can't serve two masters, at least not without a team.

Two pieces of pastoral advice rise to the surface here. The first is: Every ministry needs a champion – who is not the pastor. This simply restates the common, but constantly forgotten, trope: pastors are called to equip others for ministry, not to do ministry *for* others. The corollary advice is equally important: every champion needs a team: at minimum, three other humans who are equally invested in the ministry's faithfulness, desirability, and viability. Even Jesus sent out his disciples in pairs (Mark 6:7). In the case of Christian social innovation, capacity is not just a matter of workload. Multiple people bring multiple gifts to a project, which means everyone gets to play to their strengths. There is no faster route to burnout than doing what you don't love and aren't good at for too long.

We burn out our ministry's champions at our own peril; they are the ones who inspire others to take part. Small churches feel this most quickly, of course, but no volunteer wants to work with a burned-out champion, and no burned-out champion has the heart to joyfully develop more volunteers or train more employees. We needed a succession plan from the moment *The Feed Truck's* champion arrived, because once the champion burns out, it's too late.

Also (note to self): food trucks are seasonal businesses. And this is New Jersey.

Swimming Lessons

The Feed Truck was one of ministry's penguins: it should have worked, but it didn't. Does that make it a wasted effort? Hardly. After hundreds of thousands of years, flightless arctic birds learned that, if the air wasn't for them, the water was – and they learned to swim by using their wings as flippers. *The Feed Truck's* stationery status over the past three years has given us a base from which to experiment with new ways to use our wings. Instead of being a vehicle (literally) that brings ministry to others, it has been a laboratory for showering grace on our church's own neighborhood instead. It forced us to ask: "How might we use this unexpected asset in our parking lot to swim instead of to fly?"

Until COVID-19, *The Feed Truck's* second act was as a neighborhood event venue. Volunteers built a "big front porch" with a stage and tables by the truck's serving window, which became a place neighbors and church members gathered, often with live music (and occasionally hand-crafted egg sandwiches), to have an "unexpectedly delightful experience" of church. It was a portal for grace in a parking lot, forcing us to exercise our missional wings in different ways.

The third act of *The Feed Truck* is unknown. As I write this, conversations are underway with another congregation, a larger church with an established hunger ministry and an actual budget for a food truck, that wants to buy it. What *The Feed Truck* taught us – mistakes and all – is that innovating for love does not depend on any one form ministry might take. It depends on how we decide to use our wings.

That's how love works.

Instructions:
Read the case study.

Discuss:
- Have you ever had a big dream for ministry flop? Tell about a ministry penguin in your own congregation.

- How did your penguin learn to swim? What parts of the "body of Christ" did you notice evolving in new ways?

- Which of the lessons learned from *The Feed Truck* might be a risk for your new ministry? How will you work through it?

References for Insets

Chapter One:

Genesis

- Lizzie Crook, "Floating Genesis Church Crowned by Luminous Pop-up Roof," *deZeen* (October 30, 2020), https://www.dezeen.com/2020/10/30/genesis-floating-church-canal-boat-denizen-works-london/ (accessed May 1, 2021).

- Oliver Wainwright, "The Floating Church: Inside the Holy Vessel Bringing Salvation to Hackney Hipsters," The Guardian (October 19, 2020), https://www.theguardian.com/artanddesign/2020/oct/19/floating-church-holy-vessel-salvation-hackney-hipsters-genesis-london-olympic-park (accessed March 13, 2021).

Go Fish!

- "Go Fish!" and the Rev. Matt McNelly (interview), *Entrepreneurial Youth Ministry* (February 3, 2017), http://www.youthministryinnovators.com/blog/2017/2/13/innovators-guest-post-8-go-fish-and-rev-matt-mcnelly (accessed May 1, 2021)

- Website: https://www.gofishppc.org/about

Conetoe Family Life Center

- "A Community Grows Itself Out of Poverty," *Faith and Leadership* (October 6, 2015), https://faithandleadership.com/community-grows-its-way-out-poverty (accessed March 13, 2021).

- Jenn Lukens, "The Reverend's Revolution: A Kid-First Approach to Community Health," *The Rural Monitor* (June 29, 2016), https://www.ruralhealthinfo.org/rural-monitor/reverend-joyner-community-health/ (accessed March 13, 2021).

- Website: https://conetoelife.org/

Chapter Two:

Growing Change

- "He's Flipping a Prison Into a Farm: Meet Noran Sanford," *The State of Things*, WUNC 91.5 (September 24, 2018), https://www.wunc.org/show/the-state-of-things/2018-09-24/hes-flipping-a-prison-into-a-farm-meet-noran-sanford#stream/0 (accessed May 1, 2021).

- Wendy Bechtold, "Shoulder to Shoulder: How North Carolina Teens Are Converting a Former Jail into a Working Farm," *Sierra* (October 6, 2014), https://www.sierraclub.org/sierra/2014-6-november-december/act/shoulder-shoulder (accessed May 1, 2021).

- Marti Maguire, "Noran Sanford Turns Youthful Lives Around On Old Prison Grounds," *The News and Observer* (March 11, 2017), https://www.newsobserver.com/news/local/crime/article137946343.html (accessed May 1, 2021).

- Website: http://www.growingchange.org

The Changemaker Initiative

- "The Changemaker Initiative," Los Altos United Methodist Church website, https://laumc.org/changemaker-initiative/

- Website: https://thechangemakerinitiative.org/

Black Church Food Security Network

- Leilani Clark, "Black Churches, Powerful Cultural Forces Set Their Sites on Food Security," *Civil Eats* (July 9, 2018), https://civileats.com/2018/07/09/black-churches-powerful-cultural-forces-set-their-sights-on-food-security/ (accessed April 1, 2021).

- Edie Gross, "A Network of Black Farmers and Black Churches Delivers Fresh Food from Soil to Sanctuary," *Faith and Leadership* (May 28, 2019), https://faithandleadership.com/network-black-farmers-and-black-churches-delivers-fresh-food-soil-sanctuary (accessed April 1, 2021)

- Website: https://blackchurchfoodsecurity.net/

The Parish Collective

- Lauren Goldbloom, "The Bench on Oak Street," Parish Collective blog (June 7, 2020), https://parishcollective.org/stories-2/the-bench-on-oak-street/ (accessed April 20, 2021).

- Tim Soerens: "Where Is the Church on Tuesday Afternoon?" *Faith and Leadership* (September 1, 2020), https://faithandleadership. com/tim-soerens-where-church-tuesday-afternoon

- Website: https://parishcollective.org/about/

Chapter Three:

Mortar

- Andy Brownfield, "Two Mortar Co-Founders Stepping Down to Pursue New Businesses," *Cincinnati Business Courier* (October 30, 2020), https://www.bizjournals.com/cincinnati/news/2020/10/30/ two-mortar-co-founders-stepping-down.html (accessed May 1, 2021)

- Trina Edwards, "Web Site Names OTR 'Most Dangerous,' *Fox19 News* (June 22, 2009), https://www.fox19.com/story/10573157/ web-site-names-otr-most-dangerous/

- Ray Marcano, "MORTAR's Entrepreneur Training Helps Longtime Residents Ride the Wave of Revitalization," *Faith and Leadership* (September 4, 2018), https://faithandleadership.com/mortars-entrepreneur-training-helps-longtime-residents-ride-wave-revitalization (accessed May 1, 2021)

- Website: https://wearemortar.com/media/

The Dinner Party

- Handbook: Becca Bernstein, ed., "Making It Through Together: Ritual Collection for Life after Loss," https://static1.squarespace. com/static/5b1066184611a029fec8f7c4/t/5fd90ec7d927c34ff 5eb5739/1608060620553/Ritual+Collection+Life+After+Loss_ TheDinnerParty.pdf

- Angie Thurston and Casper ter Kuile, "How We Gather (Part 3): The Dinner Party," *On Being.* (August 19, 2016), https://onbeing.org/ blog/how-we-gather-part-3-the-dinner-party/ (accessed May 1, 2021)

- Website: https://www.thedinnerparty.org/

The People's Supper

- Caitlin Gibson, "What Happens When Two Immigrants, Five Liberals, and a Trump Voter Sit Down for Dinner," *The Washington Post* (March 17, 2017)

- https://www.washingtonpost.com/lifestyle/style/what-happens-when-two-immigrants-five-liberals-and-a-trump-voter-sit-down-to-dinner/2017/03/17/3752355c-08da-11e7-93dc-00f9bdd74ed1_story.html?utm_term=.ebb4729877da (accessed May 1, 2021)

- Website: https://thepeoplessupper.org/about-us

Union Coffee

- Zoee Acosta, "Dallas Just Got a New Hidden Two-Story Coffee Shop with a Giant Outdoor Space," (July 10, 2019), https://www.narcity.com/dallas/union-is-a-massive-coffee-shop-that-just-opened-in-dallas (accessed May 1, 2021)

- Taylor Adams, "While Awaiting Its New Location, Union Offers Coffee and Fellowship from a Truck," *Dallas Observer* (September 12, 2018), https://www.dallasobserver.com/restaurants/union-coffee-in-dallas-takes-its-religious-coffee-shop-on-wheels-11130191 (accessed May 1, 2021)

- "Union Coffee Brightens the Day for Other Dallas Nonprofits," *DallasVoice* (April 17, 2020), https://dallasvoice.com/union-coffee-brightens-day-for-other-non-profits/ (accessed May 1, 2021)

- Website: https://www.uniondallas.org/

Still Waters Landing

- Glenn Daman (Nov 30, 2020), *The Forgotten Church: Musings on the State of Rural Ministry* (Moody, 2018). Excerpted in *Sapientia* (November 30, 2020), https://henrycenter.tiu.edu/2020/11/the-forgotten-church-musings-on-the-state-of-rural-ministry/ (accessed March 13, 2021).

- Meg Gaston, "Still Waters Landing – Harvesting a God-Sized Dream," Western North Carolina Conference (The United Methodist Church) website, July 15, 2020, https://wnc-www.brtsite.com/newsdetail/still-waters-landing-harvesting-a-god-sized-dream-14129688 (accessed March 13, 2021)

- Ben Winchester, interview, University of Minnesota Extension Office, August 30, 2017 https://www.youtube.com/watch?v=-pu2FWdGqZs (accessed March 13, 2021).

- Website: https://www.stillwaterslanding.org/about-us

GoodLands

- Teresa Berger, St. Thomas More Catholic Chapel and Center at Yale University (Fall 2019), https://stm.yale.edu/molly-burhans-mapping-the-roman-catholic-church (accessed May 1, 2021).

- David Owen, "How a Young Activist Is Helping Pope Francis Battle Climate Change," *The New Yorker* (February 8, 2021), https://www.newyorker.com/magazine/2021/02/08/how-a-young-activist-is-helping-pope-francis-battle-climate-change (accessed May 1, 2021).

- Website: https://good-lands.org/

Conclusion

Nuns and Nones

- Nellie Bowles, "These Millennials Got New Roommates. They're Nuns," *The New York Times* (May 31, 2019), https://www.nytimes.com/2019/05/31/style/milliennial-nuns-spiritual-quest.html (accessed May 1, 2021)

- McKinley Corbley, "After Nuns and Millennials Discover They're 'Soul-Mates,' They Work and Live Together to Change the World," *Good News Network* (June 16, 2019),

- https://www.goodnewsnetwork.org/after-nuns-and-millennials-discover-theyre-soul-mates-they-work-and-live-together-to-change-the-world/ (accessed May 1, 2021)

- Soli Salgado, "Nuns and Nones: A Modern Religious Community," *Global Sisters Report* (February 7, 2019) https://www.globalsistersreport.org/news/trends/nuns-and-nones-modern-religious-community-55831 (accessed May 1, 2021)

Try Pie Bakery

- Melody Parker, "Try Pie Bakery Opens Storefront Location on Saturday in Waterlook" *The Courier* (November 30, 2018), https://wcfcourier.com/business/local/try-pie-bakery-opens-storefront-location-on-saturday-in-waterloo/article_1c0b1c61-3f7e-5de9-872f-ad1cb5655dcf.html (accessed April 1, 2021).

- Website: https://www.trypie.org/

Appendices

Embrace

- "Lessons From 50 Startups: Stanford Grads' *Embrace Innovations* Built Low-Cost Warmer to Save Young Indian Lives," *The Economic Times*, n.d., (https://economictimes.indiatimes.com/small-biz/startups/lessons-from-50-startups-stanford-grads-embrace-innovations-build-low-cost-warmer-to-save-young-indian-lives/printarticle/15050766.cms

- "How Jane Chen Built a Better Baby Warmer and a Thriving Business," TED Blog (July 18, 2016), https://blog.ted.com/how-jane-chen-built-a-better-baby-warmer-and-a-thriving-business/ (accessed March 1, 2021)

- Jane Chen, "How I Surfed the Wave That Nearly Drowned My Startup," *Forbes* (July 7, 2016), https://www.forbes.com/sites/janechen/2016/07/07/how-i-surfed-the-wave-that-nearly-drowned-my-startup/?sh=19fa531b136c (accessed May 1, 2021)

The Brain Kitchen

- Alan Miller, "The Brain Kitchen: A Recipe to Address Childhood Trauma," *Faith in Public Life* (August 23, 2016), http://www.iwupresident.com/the-brain-kitchen-a-recipe-to-address-childhood-trauma/ (accessed March 1, 2021).

- Robert King, "Non-profit Helps Kids Manage Trauma and Learn Coping Skills for Life," *Faith and Leadership* (May 16, 2017), https://faithandleadership.com/non-profit-helps-kids-manage-trauma-and-learn-coping-skills-life (accessed March 1, 2021).

- Tim Tedeschi, "The Brain Kitching in the Running for $25,000 Grant," *Chronicle-Tribune* (September 4, 2020), https://www.chronicle-tribune.com/news/the-brain-kitchen-in-running-for-25-000-grant/article_86bf5e78-606f-5dec-9af0-9fa1460f4332.html (accessed March 1, 2021).

- Website: https://www.thebrainkitchen.org/

The Wilmington Kitchen Collective at Grace Church

- Personal conversation with the Rev. Chelsea Spyres, July 15, 2021.

- Holly Quinn, "A Kitchen Incubator Is Coming to Wilmington," *Technical.ly* (October 1, 2020), https://technical.ly/delaware/2020/10/01/kitchen-incubator-downtown-wilmington-alliance-grace-church-food-entrepreneurs/

- Websites: https://www.wilmingtonkitchencollective.com/about-us http://www.riverfrontwilmo.com/about